Caught in between

The story of an Arab Palestinian Christian Israeli

RIAH ABU EL-ASSAL
Bishop of Jerusalem

First published in Great Britain in 1999
SPCK, Holy Trinity Church, Marylebone Road,
London NW1 4DU

Scripture extracts are from *The New Revised Standard Version of the Bible* © 1989.

British Library Cataloguing-in-Publication Data
A catalogue record for this book is available from the British Library

ISBN 0-281-05223-9

Photoset by Wilmaset Ltd, Birkenhead, Wirral
Printed in Great Britain by Caledonian International, Glasgow

Caught in between

Riah Abu El-Assal was born in 1937, to a Christian family of Nazareth. At the age of 12, and following the Declaration of the State of Israel when they had fled to Lebanon, he returned on foot to reclaim his family's home.

Both in seminary and since ordination in 1966, he has also specialized in Islamic Studies. During 32 years as priest in Nazareth, he has actively sought, through church, politics and diplomacy, for peaceful resolution of conflict in the Middle East. He was installed in 1998 as Bishop of the Diocese of Jerusalem and the Middle East.

Bishop Riah and his wife Suad have a son and two daughters.

To all who commit themselves to the task of reconciliation.

In memory of my father, Hanna, who believed in the ultimate victory of good, truth and peace.

To Mom, Muhji, who continues to uphold me in her prayers.

To my wife, Suad, who shares my pains and my hopes.

And to my children, Hanna, Lorraine, and Rania, for their wonderful love, patience and support.

Contents

CONTENTS

Foreword

Bishop Riah Abu El-Assal was enthroned as the Anglican Diocesan Bishop in Jerusalem on 15 August 1998. There was standing room only in the newly renovated St George's Cathedral as he received his crosier from retiring Bishop Samir Kafity.

So began a new chapter not only in Riah's personal and public life in Palestine/Israel, but also in the life of the Anglican Church in Jerusalem, the Middle East Council of Churches, and the Anglican Communion.

Bishop Riah has lived the majority of his life either as a refugee or under political occupation. This has had an immense impact on his theology and his understanding of church; it has influenced his world view, and the way in which he responds to events as a son, husband, father, politician, priest, bishop and friend. Nazareth has been a part of 'Israel proper' since 1948, and the residents of Nazareth are citizens of Israel, but Palestinians living in the Galilee have experienced and still experience discrimination. They may not technically be living under occupation like their brothers and sisters in the West Bank (now the Palestinian National Authority), but no Palestinian in Nazareth feels he or she enjoys all the rights and privileges of citizenship of Israel.

Caught In Between gives us the unique insight of a man who defines himself as an 'Arab, Palestinian, Christian, Israeli'. We first met when I became Dean of St George's College in Jerusalem in 1983. Every course programme included a visit to the 'home town of Jesus', and if it were possible, we would worship on a Sunday morning at Christ Church, Nazareth, where Riah served for 28 years. I would introduce him to our course members as the

'Rector of Nazareth' because he was the only cleric in Nazareth who held that title. He was always challenging, instantly breaking down stereotypes by presenting a story most Christians had not heard. When people referred to the Holy Land, he would gently correct them. For as the Prophets of old called ancient Israel to a higher sense of justice and peace, Riah calls the people of Palestine/Israel today, and the people in the world-wide family of faith, to a justice and peace for all the peoples who share the land of Israel/Palestine. Until that happens, Riah contends, the land can only be called 'the land of the Holy One'.

Riah has been accused of being anti-Semitic – although Palestinians are Semitic – and anti-Israel – although he works passionately for peace for the Israelis and even ran for the Knesset (and was roundly criticized by the Palestinian church for doing so).

In January 1993, however, I caught a glimpse of what lay at the heart of Riah's ministry. The Revd Carol Anderson, rector of All Saints' Church, Beverly Hills, California, had brought some forty pilgrims to the college, and it was decided to start their course in Nazareth by celebrating Sunday Eucharist at Christ Church. What Riah did not know at the time was that one of the pilgrims was a person by the name of Fred Rheinstein. A film producer, born a Jew, Fred had been attending All Saints' Church for many years. He had decided that, when he reached Jerusalem, he would be baptized.

When the congregation receives the Eucharist at Christ Church, everyone encircles the altar to signify the unity of the Body of Christ. As Riah distributed the bread that Sunday morning, Fred put his arms across his chest to show that he was not going to receive the Sacrament because he had not yet been baptized. Normally a priest would simply give a blessing and move on. But not Riah. Instead he embraced Fred and gave him the kiss of peace, Palestinian style!

No one from All Saints' will ever forget Riah giving his brother Jew a hug. That kiss of peace said it all. Always the reconciler, always the person struggling for justice, always the man from Nazareth, or as Riah loves to say, one of the Living Stones.

In *Caught In Between* we are given the opportunity to encounter

the thirteenth Anglican Bishop of Jerusalem. But far more importantly, we are given the opportunity to 'meet the Nazarene'.

John L. Peterson
Secretary General of the Anglican Communion
Advent 1 1998

Acknowledgements

I wish to thank all of you who have expended much effort in helping; particularly Yvonne Bearne, without whom there would simply be no book; Karen White, who was first to challenge me to tell my story; and Andrew Carey, for editing the manuscript. For the many who have supported and encouraged this project, thank you! The list would be too long to mention each individual, but know that you are loved and your efforts will long be remembered.

Introduction

On Monday, 13 September 1993, brimming with joy, I wrote the
following words to friends and brothers and sisters in Christ:

Good Monday

This is the day that the Lord has made;
Let us rejoice and be glad in it.
(Psalm 118.24)

This is truly a day for rejoicing. A day when all church bells
should ring out; when prayer calls should sing from every
mosque. It is a day to mark with celebration as we watch the two
parties formerly at war come to the table to sign an agreement
for the future.

With today's signed agreement and formal mutual recognition
of Israel and the PLO the Palestinian people have been allowed
the right, under witness of the whole world, to be recognized as
a people, with a history, a future, a legitimate source of hope.

Such a small step it might seem, yet two weeks ago it seemed
impossible. With this first wall of impossibility broken down,
there is no end to the possibilities which now open up to hope.

Now at least there is a future to look towards, whereas before
there was only fear. What a future it promises to be! The next
important step will be to move towards the federation or
confederation between Israel and Palestine. Those deprived of a
homeland who decide to come back to Palestine will be allowed
to come back. Economic development, rebuilding communities,
urban planning, agriculture, technology: so many of the region's
needs which had been displaced in the past by military

objectives, will again flourish. As trust grows hope develops, resources given to armies will go back to the community, building more hope and encouraging more investment in a spiral of development and peace.

No one could have been more pleased than myself when, just as the first draft of this book reached completion, the miraculous news came to me that the Israeli government had been meeting with representatives of the PLO in Oslo, and the two peoples who share this land which we know as the Holy Land could, at long last, hope for peace. In particular, I hope that, through this now lengthy peace process, people like myself, Israeli citizens of Palestinian origin, will finally be able to find peace within themselves. This is the question which I wanted to address in writing my book.

People may ask why did I call that Monday, 13 September 1993, Good Monday. I meant to remind people of Good Friday. In the Middle East that Friday is never referred to as Good. People speak of it either as Great Friday or as Sad Friday. I thought that that Monday was going to be both sad and good, in the sense that that handshake witnessed by millions all over the world was a great one. On Sunday, 11 December 1994 – the day after Chairman Arafat, Deputy Prime Minister Shimon Peres and the late Prime Minister Rabin received the Nobel Prize – I was asked to preach at the Chapel of the King's Palace. I discovered, in referring to Good Monday, that Scandinavians never referred to that Friday as Good, Sad or Great, but as Long. I thought then that the title I had given my message served the purpose even better: it is going to be partly sad, certainly long, but ultimately great and good.

Many visitors to Christ Evangelical Episcopal Church, Nazareth, have asked about my life as a native Nazarene and priest of this parish for the past 32 years. I often tell them (I trust you will forgive the chutzpah of the comparison) that Christians who have difficulty understanding the concept of the Trinity will best understand how I feel about my own identity. I am a citizen of the State of Israel, and I hope that one day I shall feel a true sense of belonging to this state. My life has been spent striving to realize fully each aspect of my identity, with all its inherent tensions and paradoxes.

Experience has shown me that failure to come to terms with living as a Palestinian Arab Christian in Israel usually leads to emigration. Statistics reveal that many of us have already chosen this option. If we do not find a solution quickly, the land where our faith was born and survived for two thousand years will soon be empty of indigenous Christians. The living faith will be represented only by dead stones and their imported custodians. All my effort has been dedicated to preventing this catastrophe. My colleagues have sometimes criticized my outspokenness and my involvement in what many viewed as contradictory activities. In my defence I can only say that I have always acted from deeply held, heartfelt conviction, and as honestly as I humanly could. I am motivated by my love of Christ, and my desire to serve him and my fellow man to the best of my ability. To me my actions have always seemed straightforward and logical.

My political orientation is strongly influenced by my experience as a member of a discriminated minority, that of the Palestinian in Israel. I have worked within the Israeli political system, at one time standing for election to the *Knesset* (the Israeli Parliament), for the right of the Palestinian people to a state, side by side with Israel. At one point my support for a Palestinian state led to my being defamed as a tool of the PLO and banned from travelling abroad for four years, but I have always believed that we shall only be free to strive for equal rights for Palestinians within the State of Israel when my Palestinian brothers and sisters in exile have a homeland of their own.

Religious affiliation obviously has a special significance in a country which defines itself as the State of the Jews. Here, faith is not the private and personal affair of the individual but a declaration of belonging to a recognized community which regulates important spheres of life such as marriage and inheritance. But to my sorrow, religion is becoming an increasingly decisive factor in our region. Fundamentalist attitudes, extremes of which are represented in Israel by the Islamic group Hamas and the Jewish political party Moledet, prevail over human and national concerns. Add to this the identification of many evangelical Christians with the aims of Zionism and you have an explosive mix.

Internationally, I belong to a Communion of over 70 million

Anglicans, shepherded by nearly 800 bishops. Recently, a large majority of these bishops participated in the Lambeth Conference. Hearing the Gospel read in Arabic for the first time in Canterbury Cathedral brought great joy to my soul. This joy quickly turned into sorrow as his grace, the Archbishop of Canterbury, my good friend, made no reference to the Middle East situation in his presidential address. (The presidential address sets the agenda for similar gatherings.) As though ignorance of our present situation was not enough, the following day salt was added to the wounds of my heart. The play *Wrestling With Angels*, written especially for the conference and based on Genesis and Ezekiel, was most offensive to Arab Christians in the Holy Land. My only option was to walk out of the conference; my intentions were to return home. Upon hearing the news, the Archbishop graciously apologized to me and challenged me to stay and make the wrong right; by doing so I believed I could create a greater awareness of the real Middle East situation. Our story was covered in a positive way by major newspapers and the BBC. I continued to share throughout the remainder of the conference. My wounded heart rejoiced once again as the majority of the attending bishops responded with a resounding 'YES' to a resolution on Jerusalem and the Holy Land which many believe to be the best in the last 30 years. Returning home I counted 20 July as another Good Monday as I recalled Samson's riddle, 'Out of the eater came something to eat. Out of the strong came something sweet' (Judges 14.14). I had a lot to ponder as I prepared to be enthroned as the 13th diocesan bishop of the Anglican Diocese of Jerusalem. As I remember my Good Mondays I must also help people understand better who we are, where we are going, and why we call this Holy Land our home.

My ethnic identity is Arab. My cultural and social roots are Arab, my mother tongue is Arabic. Many pilgrims are surprised when they hear this, but I see it as one of the strong options of our special situation. As an Arab I am bound by the traditions governing our society, with their emphasis on honour and shame, and reconciliation rather than negotiation as the means to resolve conflict. I will endeavour to show how important this is for the resolution of the Arab–Israeli conflict, and how, as an

Anglican Christian educated in the European tradition, I believe that I and others like me are optimally placed to serve as a bridge between 'occident' and 'orient'.

Riah Abu El-Assal

one *Home sweet home*

I will say to the Lord, 'My refuge and my fortress'. (PSALM 91.2)

On the plane I chatted to my neighbour, a pleasant-spoken American who was headed for the early-warning air-base set up by the United States in Sinai under the Egyptian–Israeli peace treaty. As the plane taxied to a halt he remarked enviously that I would be at home and in bed before he was halfway to his base in the desert. He eyed me doubtfully when I replied that he would probably be at home before I had even left the airport.

As we left the plane he insisted that I go first, out of deference to my calling. Thus he was behind me as we went down the steps and across the tarmac towards the waiting shuttle bus, and he saw the Israeli soldier come forward to meet me. I turned and waved to him before the soldier took my arm and led me to an army vehicle waiting on the tarmac. I wondered what my American friend was thinking now.

Tiredly I pulled my thoughts together and faced the questioning I knew would follow.

'What's your name? Where do you live? What's your father's name, your grandfather's name, your brother's . . . ? What is your business? The name of your church? Tell me something about Nazareth. Where is your house located? Where does your mother live? Her date of birth? Where have you been? Why did you go there? Did you bring anything with you? A gift for someone? A message?'

To this last I replied that I brought many greetings from friends abroad to my flock. I told them the security requirements of the

State of Israel were well known to me and I had not contravened any of them; it made no difference. When they asked whether I was carrying any weapons on me, the rebel in me awoke. 'Yes,' I said.

The tension was palpable. I was ordered to walk a few steps away and, at what they thought was a safe distance, directed to take out this 'weapon' – slowly. I bent to my case, opened it slowly and removed my Bible, which I held up for them to see.

It is the only weapon I have ever carried; the only one I have ever needed.

Childhood

It was my grandmother who introduced me to the Scriptures, when she told me and my brothers and sisters stories from the Old and New Testaments by the light of the petroleum lamp, as we lay in bed. She also gave me the ninety-first psalm as a pillar to lean on in time of trouble. It has served me well.

My grandmother was the second wife of my grandfather, whose first wife died after bearing him two sons. Grandmother was a childless widow when grandfather asked her to marry him. He had decided that two children were enough for him and he wanted no more. My grandmother bore him twelve daughters and my father, the thirteenth and last child.

Grandfather's house was situated in what is now the main street in Nazareth, but was then the edge of town. Beyond the house I believed that hyenas, wolves and snakes lurked to threaten unwary children who wandered off alone. He raised cattle, horses and camels and my grandmother turned part of the house into a small hotel used mainly by Christian pilgrims and *Druze** farmers who came to the market in Nazareth from the surrounding villages. My grandparents were on good terms with these guests. Indeed, at my father's funeral a Druze man introduced himself to me as my father's milk-brother. His own mother had been too sick to nurse him as a baby, so my grandmother, who was nursing my father at the time, had acted as wet-nurse to him.

Nazareth was a small, closely knit community in the 1930s. The whole populace used to turn out to celebrate weddings, and

*Terms in italics which may be unfamiliar to the reader will be found in the Glossary, p. 155.

funerals were a time of general mourning. As a boy I drank the water from Mary's Well and played with my friends and cousins on some waste ground across the road from our house. Our games were different from those of other boys only in that we did not play cops and robbers. Our gangs were the 'Jews' and the 'Arabs' – and in our games the Arabs always won.

My childhood came to an end in 1948, when I was 11 years old.

1948, Flight into Lebanon

We had a big, black Dodge, which we loaded with mattresses, food for the journey and 14 people, including my father, who was driving, my mother, sitting beside him, two aunts with their three children, and my sisters and brothers. There was not enough room for all of us inside the car, so my brother Rohi and I rode standing on the running boards, with our arms wrapped tightly round the door frames. This form of travelling had two advantages – first, it helped my car sickness, and second, Rohi and I could keep an eye on the wheels, to make sure they didn't fall off!

We crossed the border to the Lebanon. My father refused to register us as refugees. We lived off his savings and the gold my grandmother had left to my mother, which we sold in the markets of Beirut. I felt the tension. In the streets we children were exposed to the taunts of the Lebanese children, who called us *laji'een*: refugees. For reasons I didn't even understand myself, I felt that the term was humiliating, and I remember at least once getting into a fight with a boy who taunted me thus.

David Ben Gurion[1] claimed that the Palestinian Arab showed no emotional involvement in Palestine: 'Why should he? He is equally at ease whether in Jordan, Lebanon or a variety of places. They are as much his country as this is. And as little.' But it wasn't true. I wanted to go home. Bible stories had increased the significance of Nazareth in my own mind – they must have done, otherwise why would I choose to return at such a young age and in such danger and difficulty? I remembered watching pilgrims from all over the world walking towards the Grotto of the Annunciation and kneeling as they approached. All of a sudden my childhood, my playground, my school had been taken away from me. I wanted them back and I was prepared to return without my family.

3

1949, Return to Palestine

After a year in Beirut I spoke to my father. Dad was worried about the turmoil that still reigned in Palestine, but he agreed that my older sister Suad and I could go back to Nazareth together. It was illegal but we contacted a man who knew a way over the border. There were five of us crossing together. We travelled first to Rmeish, in the south of Lebanon, and then we walked to the border through the mountains. We made the crossing during the day, after a donkey carrying an illegal returnee had been shot trying to cross at night.

It was a much tougher decision for Suad to take. While I would be satisfied with a pair of sandals for winter and summer, girls of her age needed more. I still remember how much courage it took for her to make the border crossing. But she shared the same strength of feeling about Nazareth. We were the eldest, we were very close to each other and we always looked alike. As a result of our hardship and love of Nazareth there was always a very special link between us.

An old woman with us, Imm Antoin Laham, fed my sister and me biscuits during the march. I was scolded for wandering from the path to take pot-shots at the pigeons with my slingshot, which I always carried with me for such opportunities. I was a very accurate shot and we had often enjoyed a dinner of roast pigeon in Beirut. My parents were grateful for this supplement to our diet.

We walked on through the scrub on the hills of Southern Lebanon until we reached a church, which we were later to discover was the Greek Catholic (Melkite) church of Bir'am – the only building left standing in the village. Here we were given shelter while our guide went to check whether the road ahead was clear. He knew that an Israeli tank would be passing at about that time. Thus I entered Israel for the first time. I was 12 years old and Suad 13.

two *Caught in between*

Read the 'fatiha' over them.

Palestinian in Israel

I am an Israeli – or am I? I became an Israeli citizen in 1959, for the simple reason I had to go abroad if I wanted to study theology, and there was no other way I could be sure that I would be allowed to return home. Sadly, it was not an act of love.

The definition of Israel as the sovereign state of the Jews did not encourage me to look on it as my country, nor were Palestinian residents of the country wooed as citizens in the way that Jews all over the world were. In fact I realized only gradually that I was going to live in the State of Israel. When I returned to Nazareth, the town was not considered officially part of Israel.

We are so used to looking on the West Bank and the Gaza Strip today as 'the Occupied Territories' that we – even we who live here – forget that Nazareth and Galilee were part of the territory assigned to the Palestinian state by the United Nations partition plan of 1947. In spite of repeated Israeli claims that the Arab armies 'invaded Israel' in 1948, actually nearly all the fighting took place in areas assigned to the Palestinian state. These territories were effectively conquered by Israel, which incorporated about half of the designated Palestinian lands into itself. The other half was annexed by Jordan.

A cousin of mine who applied for citizenship of the United States wrote under date and place of birth on his application forms: 1956 in Nazareth, Palestine. The immigration officials objected, claiming that in 1956 Nazareth was in the State of Israel.

My cousin pointed out that Israel had been internationally recognized only within the borders of the UN partition plan of 1947,[1] and that Nazareth was not part of this territory. Thereafter, many of the younger Israeli Palestinians entering the United States or Canada entered 'Nazareth, Palestine' on their immigration forms as their place of birth, and it was accepted.

There are two classes of citizen in Israel – Jews and non-Jews. In the period immediately following the establishment of the state our identity cards still carried the word 'Palestinian' beside the term nationality. This has since been changed to 'Arab' in what is an attempt, we believe, to eradicate our identity as Palestinians. When I received my first *laissez-passer*, a travel document which allowed me to go to France in 1958, 'undetermined' was written against the term nationality, although the French allowed me to put 'Palestinian' on my immigration form.

Today any Jew, from anywhere in the world, has the right to immigrate to Israel (with one notable exception: Jews by birth who convert to Christianity forfeit this right). It is called the Right of Return. In stark contrast the non-Jewish Palestinian who was born here, who held a Palestinian passport prior to 1948, has no such right. Furthermore, all the symbols of the state are Jewish symbols – the *menorah* and the Star of David. The Israeli national anthem, *HaTikva*, was the hymn of the Zionist movement. It expresses the yearning of the Jewish people for a land of their own. It is a beautiful song, but it is not mine, and never can be.

In the Declaration on the Establishment of the State of Israel of 14 May 1948, the state was declared to be a 'Jewish State in Eretz Israel'. It would 'open its doors to every Jew and grant the Jewish people the status of a nation with equal rights among the family of nations'. Arab residents of the state were called upon to 'preserve the peace and take part in the building of the state on the footing of full and equal nationality and appropriate representation in all its organs'. But it quickly became apparent that we were under military rule, which continued until 1966. During this period travel was restricted for Arabs. We had to queue for travel permits at the Moscobiyeh if we wanted to go shopping in Haifa or swimming in the Sea of Galilee. We could travel freely only once a year – on Israel's Independence Day!

The secret service was everywhere. Anyone who needed an official permit, a licence, a new identity paper – we all needed something – was subject to pressure to spy on his neighbours. With 'collaboration' so widespread it was easy to spread rumours about anyone you had a personal grudge against. Fear and mistrust grew like a fungus in a dark, damp cellar.

Even after the lifting of military rule in 1966, pressure was put on people to spy on their neighbours. Our parish treasurer was asked to report on my activities to the *Shin Beth*. As he was already retired and had no job to lose, he was able to tell them openly that he had no intention of doing any such thing, and immediately came and told me about it. I discovered that my parishioners in Nazareth and in Reineh, a village close to Nazareth which was also in my charge, had been asked to record my sermons and pass them to the Shin Beth.

Luckily it seems my preaching was not potent enough to influence these agents of the state, or I might have been charged with breaking the conversion law, which forbids missionary activity in Israel! We felt claustrophobic, as though George Orwell's enclosed and intrusive vision in *1984* had been transposed from the dark and drizzle of London, to the light and sun of Nazareth.

As if Israeli intelligence activity was not enough, military governors were installed by the minister of defence to control the Negev (Military Government Southern Area), the Triangle[2] (Military Government Central Area) and Galilee (Military Government Northern Area), i.e. all those areas where Arabs were still in the majority.[3] They applied emergency laws passed by the British Mandate government in 1945 and the Israeli Defence Law of 1949. These laws applied in theory to all the citizens of the state; they were in fact only used against Arab citizens. Even the state comptroller (the Israeli ombudsman) in his report on the Ministry of Defence for the financial period 1957–9 found that: 'There is something improper about this law, which was drafted with the intention of its being applicable to all the inhabitants of the country, whereas in fact it is only enforced against some of them.'

Such laws made life in Nazareth irksome. It was difficult for Palestinians to find work, because we needed a permit to leave the town. Going shopping in Haifa meant queuing for a travel permit, which was often issued for such a short period that it was difficult to get there and back in the time allowed. Swimming in the Sea of Galilee was impossible, because Tiberias was a closed military area (being near the border with Jordan), and thus we could not go there at all. Under Article 125 of the Defence Laws any area could be declared closed, but for 'security reasons' the precise frontiers of these closed areas were known to no one except the staff of the military government. Citizens who wished to leave or enter these areas were forced to go each time to a police station – which often could not provide the information – or to the officers of the military government, which were few and far between. However, leaving or entering a closed area without permission led to prosecution for breaking the Defence Laws, and not knowing where the boundaries were did not protect a person from prosecution. This was not so important if we only wanted to go swimming, but it could happen that a farmer suddenly found his fields were in a closed area and he was forbidden to go to them.

In the early years of the state, civil and military police used regularly to board buses and order Arab passengers out for inspection of their identity cards and travel permits. Apart from the indignity of such treatment, being discovered without a permit led to harsh fines or even detention for a few hours or days for being either inside or outside a closed area without the appropriate pass.

The military governor could issue an administrative order for police supervision, including supervision of a person's professional work. These articles were used against journalists in particular. A person under police supervision had to remain indoors between sunset and sunrise, and the police had the right of access to his home at any hour of the day or night. Anyone could be detained for an unlimited period without trial, or he could be expelled from the country or banished to a remote place far from his home, where he had no accommodation and no means of earning a living for himself and his family. To make his situation even more difficult he might be required to report daily to a police station 20 kilometres away.

A particularly cruel instance of such an order was issued against Ahmad Hassan, a bedouin who lived near the village of Araba, who was ordered to sit every day for six months, from sunrise to sunset, under a large carob tree which stands to the west of the village of Deir Hanna.

Another article allowed the military government to impose a total or partial curfew in any village or area. A curfew was imposed on almost all the villages of the Triangle for most of the night for 14 years, at first from 9 p.m. to 5 a.m., then from 10 p.m. to 4 a.m. The military government had the right to enforce these laws whenever it was required 'to ensure the safety of the people, the security of Israel, the maintenance of public order...', which gave it a lot of scope.

It was claimed this was necessary for the security of the state, but in fact, years before it was eventually lifted, the majority of Israel's intellectual and political leaders realized that in fact it damaged the security of the state, because it frustrated and angered the Arab population and reminded them constantly that they were not equal citizens. Military government was eventually lifted in 1966, but the Defence Laws were not repealed then. In fact, even as late as 1990 I was a victim of one of them, as we shall see.

Arab citizens are constantly made to feel that they are outsiders, but perhaps the most effective area of exclusion is military service. Every citizen of Israel from the age of 18, male and female, can be called on to serve in the armed forces. The armed forces are the melting-pot of Israel. During their service men and women from all walks of life and from all countries are thrown together. It is – at least theoretically – the time when they learn to respect each other and to forge bonds. Non-Jewish citizens, with the exception of the Druze, are not called up. Bedouin and Christian Arabs can volunteer for military service. Bedouins have served in the armed forces for many years.

The acceptance of Christian soldiers is a relatively new development, and one which many Arab citizens view as an attempt to drive a wedge between segments of the Arab population. Until very recently, it was rare for Christians to volunteer, but under the current economic pressures they are beginning to do so in greater numbers. Few Muslim Arabs, with the exception of the Druze and bedouin minorities, have been admitted to the Israeli Defence Forces (IDF).

This is one of the rare spheres where Jews and Arabs are largely in accord. As long as the main task of the Israeli army was to sub-jugate Palestinians in Israel and the Occupied Territories, as long as the Israeli airforce continued to bomb Palestinian refugee camps in Lebanon, there is no way I or my children could serve them. Military service is the great divider. Jobs are advertised for those who have served in the IDF. Mortgages are cheaper for those who have served in the forces. Children's allowances are higher for those who have served in the forces. Those who have served in the armed forces are to be preferred for entrance to uni-versities and occupational training courses run by the state. They receive loans to pay the fees for higher education.

Even as recently as 1991 in the build-up to the 1991 Gulf War, gas masks were distributed first to those who had served in the IDF; then to Arab citizens and much later, under international pressure, to Palestinians in the Occupied Territories.

THE SINAI CAMPAIGN

I remember vividly an experience during an earlier war, the Sinai campaign of 1956. I was only 19 and training to be a teacher at the Baptist Village near Petah Tikva. We were two students from Nazareth. One of the Baptist missionaries came to us and told us that it would be better if we went home for the duration of the war. The two of us went into Petah Tikva to find a bus to take us to Haifa, from where we would continue to Nazareth.

There were hardly any people on the streets. More especially there were no young men, because they were all at the front. Some of the women we met started cursing us, asking why we weren't in the army with the rest of them, telling us we should be ashamed of ourselves. Usually we did not respond, fearing that they would realize we were Arabs, but once I muttered in Hebrew that we were on our way back to base. We were terrified that the prevailing anti-Arab feelings would lead to some kind of attack on us. It was an eerie feeling and one which would be repeated, with variations, in every subsequent war between Israel and its Arab neighbours.

In fact 1956 proved to be a very important year for Arab Israelis. Many of us realized that we had misjudged the strength of the state when we saw how Israel negotiated with Britain and France over their claims to the Suez Canal. They dealt with the Western superpowers in a way which was quite new to us and very impressive. But during this campaign thousands of Arabs – Israeli citizens – were expelled from Galilee. The former Prime Minister of Israel, Yitzhak Rabin, was commander of the northern region at the time. He himself revealed that between three and five thousand people were expelled to Syria by the army, after they had been driven from their native villages in 1951 in the course of water diversion projects.[4]

Something else happened during the Sinai campaign which filled us with fear and brought home to us that we were not accepted in Israel. This was the massacre in Kufr Qassem, an Arab village located near the road to Jerusalem. On 29 October a curfew was declared without warning. This happened quite often. The men out working in the fields heard nothing about it and came home at the end of the day. Forty-nine of them were shot dead by soldiers of the frontier guard. One woman was shot when she rushed out of her house to help her husband, who had been wounded. Her son came rushing out to help her, and he too was shot.

I heard more about the events when I returned to my teacher training course in the Baptist Village at Petah Tikva, after the campaign. The Kufr Qassem labourers who had worked on the Village farm were among those shot dead. When we returned to the Baptist Village, we found only one of them had been spared. He had seven bullet wounds, but by a miracle none of the bullets had hit a vital organ.

While the massacre was horrifying in itself, what really upset us was the sequel. The commander of the unit responsible was court-martialled and fined for his part in the massacre – 1 piaster, the symbolic equivalent of a penny! Arab life was evidently very cheap. We felt that we could be murdered or expelled from the country at any time. The situation has improved since then, but even today, at least one of the parties represented in the Knesset (Moledet) calls openly for our 'transfer' to the neighbouring Arab countries, and in Jewish towns you will find slogans reading 'Death to the Arabs' on the walls – slogans which the authorities do not rush to remove.

THE SIX DAY WAR

I was a newly married young priest in Nazareth when the 1967 so-called Six Day War broke out. I say so-called, because I do not believe that this war lasted only six days; in fact it is not over yet. For us the war meant a return to a system of permits to leave the area. Some people started hoarding food. Many Arabs in Israel believed that Nasser would win the war. He was viewed as a giant among leaders.

Yet our feelings were very mixed. Military rule had just been lifted. Until then we had considered ourselves under Israeli occupation. Now we were Israelis, with the Syrian army on one side and the Egyptian army on the other. My wife's uncle, the writer Emile Habiby, who was a leading member of the Israeli Communist Party and a Member of the Knesset, came to ask us to hide him. I was amazed that he really feared that the Israeli government would round up Arab leaders in Israel.

'Why should they want to do that?' I asked him. He told me that one of his friends in the Knesset, a Jew, had told him of Israeli plans to put Israeli Arabs between themselves and the advancing Arab armies in case of a military defeat. As a prominent Israeli Arab he had reason to believe that he might be in particular danger.

When I asked Emile if he really believed in such a plan, he reminded me how his comrades from the Communist Party, and other Arab friends who were not members of the party, were jailed during the Sinai campaign of 1956. Then, his parliamentary immunity had saved him, but the memory of Jewish brutality to Israeli Arabs in 1956, especially the deportations and the massacre of innocent Arabs in Kufr Qassem, had made him determined to take no chances. A war which reached Israeli territory would have meant that we were crushed between the two sides, belonging to both and to neither.

Our situation was brought painfully into focus by President Nasser. When asked what would happen to the Palestinians in Israel if the Arabs won the war he replied, 'Read the *fatiha* over them.' The *fatiha* is a *sura* from the Qur'an which is read at funerals.

Being an Arab

Some Palestinians in Israel try to avoid this conflict by hiding their nationality. Those of us who grew up in mixed areas, where both Jews and Arabs live, usually speak Hebrew without an Arabic accent. For these people it is tempting to speak Hebrew in public, even among themselves. I was shocked when I went to Haifa in the Fifties to work in a carpenter's shop in the school holidays. I became friends with a fellow Christian from Haifa, Jeryis. We were strolling through the city together one day, when some young Jews hailed us, calling 'Hey, Gershon, how are things?' They came and chatted to my friend for a while.

'And who's this?' asked a young man, eyeing me.

'I'm Riah,' I replied.

'Riah? What kind of name's that?' he asked.

'I'm an Arab, from Nazareth,' I said.

When we moved off I looked at Jeryis. 'What's all this "Gershon" business?' I asked.

He shrugged and looked shamefaced. 'I call myself Gershon around here,' he said, 'it saves explanations and I get further with a Jewish name. How do you think I got my job? And anyway, they have some nice girls, but you wouldn't catch them going out with an Arab, so . . .'

'Gershon' spoke Hebrew quite well; at least as well as the Polish Jewess he was going out with at the time. Strangely I was myself often taken for a Jew, on account of my fair hair and blue eyes! It probably sounds strange to an American or European reader, but blond hair and blue eyes signified a Jew in Palestine. My mother often had similar problems because strangers to Nazareth took her for a Jewess. It was particularly difficult for her in the 1940s when many of the Palestinian guerrillas were stationed in Nazareth. Being a Christian, she did not cover her head like most of the Muslim women did then, and she was suspected more than once of being a Jewish infiltrator.

While it was easy in moments of fear to fall into the tempting trap of pretending to be Jewish, I knew that we had to fight and continue fighting for acceptance on our own terms. There is no hiding. I cannot spend my life pretending to be what I am not.

The price is too high. 'Gershon' serves as an example to me. In spite of his willingness to deny his roots in order to be accepted in this country, it seems he failed. He emigrated to Canada, as so many have, to escape the pressures.

It was not only within Israel that we were denied recognition. Until 1967 the Arabs outside Israel had had very little idea of our life in the new state. We were widely looked on as traitors to the Palestinian cause, people who had sold out to the occupier. In 1958 my friend Riad and I were in Genoa, in Italy. Passing a street café, we overheard two men speaking Arabic and greeted them with the usual *marhaba*. We introduced ourselves and the two men asked us where we came from.

'Nazareth,' we said. They had never heard of Nazareth. 'Well, we're from Galilee,' I said.

'Where is Galilee?'

'In hm . . . er . . . in Israel.'

'You're Arabs, why do you say Israel? Why don't you say the Occupied Territories?'

'OK, if you like, the Occupied Territories.'

And the moment they discovered we were Israelis they stopped talking to us and simply left. Travelling in Europe I was often asked where I came from, and would answer truthfully 'from Israel'. I remember one particular occasion when this led to a long conversation with a Frenchman who spoke English well. We were taking the train from Marseilles to Paris, and as we left Marseilles there was an explosion in the oil refineries, which we later heard was caused by Algerian groups in France in retaliation for actions of the French in Algeria. The man kept talking about the war in Algeria, calling the Algerians 'dirty Arabs'. I'm sure he thought that as an Israeli I would sympathize with his views. When we arrived in Paris he invited me for a cup of tea or coffee and I asked him whether he really wanted to drink coffee with a 'dirty Arab'.

'What do you mean?' he asked. So I told him that I was one of those Arabs he had just been telling me about. He blushed and apologized, but I have been in such situations again and again, both in Israel and abroad.

Another experience saddened my heart. In early 1967, shortly after I was ordained, the Archbishop asked me to represent the diocese at a conference organized by the World Council of Churches in Nairobi. I must have been the first Palestinian priest from Israel ever to have been sent abroad on such a mission by the Archbishop in Jerusalem. In fact I was on the first flight to Kenya which flew over the Sinai Desert after it had fallen into Israeli hands in the Six Day War. We could see the oilfields still burning below us.

The conference, on the subject of Christian education, was attended by about 800 delegates, observers and staff, and I found it very exciting to represent my people before such a great gathering. I did not know what to expect. There were delegates from Egypt, Jordan and from Lebanon. Some of them were expatriates who, in my opinion, gave a false impression of the Arab-Christian reaction to the war. One lady from the Lebanon made me particularly angry, so much so that I interrupted her speech. She claimed that the Arab Christians were overjoyed to witness the defeat of the Arab armed forces. I told her she was endangering the lives of Arab Christians in the Middle East by speaking in this manner. I could not understand how she could talk like this. We had just been defeated in a humiliating war, and she claimed we were happy? We were far from happy.

During the conference a regional meeting was held for the people from Egypt, Syria, Jordan and Lebanon. I was introduced as Riah Abu El-Assal from Israel. When I stood up to speak the Egyptian delegate left the room. 'I will not stay in this room with an Israeli,' he said.

It was borne upon me how ignorant people were of the true situation in Israel. How ignorant of the reality of the State of Israel. Arabs from the neighbouring states viewed us as collaborators with the Zionist regime. They knew very little of the conditions under which we were struggling.

It was my impression that the Egyptians knew even less about our situation than people from the other neighbouring countries, Jordan, Lebanon and Syria, especially Syria. They did not understand that by remaining on the land and not fleeing, we had won the battle lost by the majority of our people.

three *Present absentees*

*It was not as though there was a Palestinian people in Palestine
considering itself a Palestinian people and we came and threw them
out and took their country away from them. They did not
exist.* (GOLDA MEIR)[1]

Nazareth, 1949–

Soon after our arrival in Israel my uncle took Suad and me to the
Moscobiyeh, the former Russian Orthodox seminary built in the
nineteenth century and serving at the time as the district military
governor's office. We told our story of having lost sight of our
parents in Lebanon and found our way back to the protection of
relatives in Nazareth. I don't know whether they believed us, but
we had our pictures taken and were given military identity cards.
This was not a very secure status and meant that we could be de-
ported at any time, but it was a step in the right direction. Probably
we were only given permission to stay at all because of the uncer-
tainty regarding the status of Nazareth and the surrounding area.

In 1948 the Israelis had razed the villages of Galilee to the
ground. Many of the residents of those villages fled in fear. The Palestinians in conquered villages and towns were ordered to assemble in a certain place, such as the town square, then they were
loaded into lorries and taken away. Some, from northern towns,
were brought to Nazareth. Many others made their own way
here, believing that they would be safe in Nazareth, as a holy city.

When we arrived from Lebanon, Nazareth was full of refugees –
Christians and Muslims – from Haifa, Beisan (now known as Beit

Shean), Acre, Saffouriya (the home of Elizabeth, mother of John the Baptist) and other villages only remembered because of the families who carry their name. The people of Saffouriya, which was situated about six kilometres to the north of Nazareth, built their new homes on a hill which overlooked their former village. From there they were able to watch the new town of Zippora rise out of the ruins of their old lives.

Now that I no longer needed to hide, I went to my father's house, where to my horror I was refused permission to enter.

My home was in the care of the Custodian for Absentee Property, whose task ostensibly was to look after it for the absentee owner. Gradually I learned about the Absentee Property Law. Under this law an 'absentee' is a person who was in Lebanon, Egypt, Syria, Saudi Arabia, Trans-Jordan, Iraq or Yemen at any time after 27 November 1947 (the date of the UN resolution to partition Palestine). However, it was not necessary to leave Palestine to become an 'absentee'. It was enough to leave your ordinary place of residence for a place inside Palestine 'held at that time by forces which sought to prevent the establishing of the State of Israel'.

Thus my aunt and her husband who fled from Haifa to shelter with her family in Nazareth during the fighting became 'absentees' and lost their home. However, like Suad and me, they were not absent: they were very present. We became known as the 'present absentees'.

It appears that 75,000 persons who remained in Israel after the war of 1948 became 'present absentees'.[2] Arab homes which were not destroyed were turned over to the new Jewish immigrants. In Nazareth, the expelled Palestinians lived in the pilgrims' hostels and even in the schools where we children were trying to learn. Their property remained in the hands of the Custodian for Absentee Property. Even today absentee property in Arab East Jerusalem is being sold to Jewish settlers.

Our own case was sadly and painfully different. My aunt from Haifa and her husband were living in our house. They were paying rent for it to the Custodian for Absentee Property and refused to let me in. I asked them about the furniture, and learned that we had forfeited our right to it when we left. They wouldn't even let me pick figs from our fig tree. When I tried, my aunt's husband ran after me with a stone in his hand, chasing me out of my parents' garden.

But, my father had entrusted me with the care of our home, and I wasn't going to give up without a fight. I went back to my aunt. 'Please can I at least have my marbles?' I begged, 'I hid them here before we left.' I went to the place where my father had told me I would find the little bag containing the deeds to the property, and other valuable family documents which he had hidden, and I took them with me.

Our life as 'present absentees' was not an easy one. Suad and I were living with my father's sister. She was a very kind woman, a devout Christian and well known in Nazareth, since she was the local midwife and most babies came into the world with her help. She was generally known as 'Mama'. She and her husband had a big house and my aunt was happy to take in the children of her only brother. But living with relatives, however kind they were, was not like being at home.

I tried very hard never to do anything wrong, to be independent, to take good care of my clothes and shoes in order not to be a burden on my aunt and uncle. Looking back I realize that, unhappy as I was, I learned a valuable lesson in self-reliance and discipline then.

In 1953 my mother also crossed the border illegally, bringing with her my three younger sisters and my youngest brother George, whom I had never seen. My father and my brothers Rohi and Kamal remained in Beirut. My mother and brothers and sisters also moved in with my father's sister and her husband. For people who, according to Prime Minister Golda Meir, did not exist, we took up a lot of space! However, we had nowhere else to go until fate intervened, and a third aunt, who had also been living in my parents' house, died. The Custodian for Absentee Property allowed the seven of us to move into her two rooms.

Three times my mother, who was still living in Nazareth illegally, was served a deportation order, and I prayed very hard every time that something would happen so that she need not leave. And indeed something always did happen. My mother claimed she did not know where my father was. The Mayor of Nazareth, Saifeddin Zou'abi and our pastor, Revd Khalil Jamal,[3] fought together again for the right of my mother to stay in Nazareth. After the establishment of the state, Mayor Zou'abi cooperated with the government and had some influence in governmental circles. In fact he was accused of collaboration, but although I was one of those who disagreed with him politically, I cannot deny that he was generous to a fault and my parents had reason to be grateful to him.

At a reception the Mayor gave for Moshe Sharett, the Prime Minister of Israel at the time, Revd Jamal raised the question of my mother's predicament with him. Moshe Sharett was known to be sympathetic to the Arabs of Israel. In his memoirs he recalls how he tried to persuade the Palestinians not to leave Haifa in 1948. He promised to help.

Finally, in 1955, my mother was given leave to stay. The news came at the last minute, when she and the children were literally sitting on packed suitcases. We continued to live in our two rooms, for which we had to pay rent, although my father had inherited a half share in the house and bought the property outright in 1937, the year of my birth. When I presented the documents to the Custodian in Nazareth, he agreed to pay my school fees with part of the rent from the house. In his own way he was kind to me, and I am grateful for his help; but the property was not released until after my father returned from Lebanon in 1958. Even so, when it was finally released the Custodian demanded a large sum of money from us to cover the cost of administering the property.

We still could not evict my aunt and her family, who had become protected tenants. I confess it gave me pleasure to invite my friends around every evening for a drum practice session, until they left 'voluntarily'. And I am still here, more present than absent, in spite of the cost. In fact I am proud to say that I have been able to make my presence felt quite often.

Claiming the land

As a rural people the Palestinians have always been attached to their land, but at the end of the nineteenth century some of the poorer people and wealthy landlords started to sell land to the Jewish immigrants who offered high prices for it. They little realized that they were selling not just their farmland but their homeland.

When the State of Israel was established in 1948 only 5.67 per cent of the land in Palestine was owned by Jews. The new state began a massive programme of expropriation, in the course of which 374 Palestinian villages were demolished,[4] although even today evidence of their existence can be found. The observant visitor to the country who looks into the newly planted pine forests will see, even from the road, cactus hedges and olive trees which signify that here was once an Arab village. Closer inspection will reveal lemon trees and vines denoting former gardens. Of the buildings, only the mosques and churches were left standing.

Fifty per cent of the municipal area of Nazareth and the lands of the neighbouring villages, Ein Mahel and Reineh, were confiscated to build what is now the new town of Nazareth Illit (Upper Nazareth), as part of a process known as the Judaization of Galilee. No one can purchase confiscated land outright. It is transferred to the Jewish Land Fund, which leases it under 99-year leaseholds. Under this system land is occasionally leased to its previous (Arab) owners, as happened in Saffouriya. Usually it is leased to Jewish tenants and developers.

Before the establishment of the State of Israel, Nazareth had two thriving factories, one for cigarettes and one for matches. Both closed in the Fifties (to my personal satisfaction, since I dislike smoking intensely!) because they could not compete with subsidized industries in the Jewish sector. At the same time hundreds of small and four large industries were established in Upper Nazareth, with the aim of providing work for the Jewish immigrants. These factories are built on the lands of Nazareth, Reineh and Ein Mahel, which now hardly have an acre outside their built-up areas. The villagers have become the new proletariat. In spite of the government, they have found jobs in the factories built on what used to be their land. Needless to say they are employed in menial and poorly paid tasks.

Since 1948 the Israeli government has confiscated 93 per cent of the land which previously belonged to Arab Palestinians, much of it under the Absentee Property Law; but many laws have been enacted since 1948 to legalize the expropriation of land.

Later, my own sister Suad and her husband became victims of one of these laws when the government decided to build Nazareth Illit. My brother-in-law, Ghassan Musmar, lived as a child with his father, mother and four brothers and sisters on a smallholding just outside Nazareth. Ghassan's father had worked for some time in Germany and returned with enough money to set up a pottery, making earthenware water-jars and pots. He discovered that the clay soil on which he lived was ideal for making such earthenware. With the help of Ghassan's mother, Julia, who planted and tended the fruit and vegetables, he produced enough on the farm to feed his family, and the little pottery provided a cash income. Life continued in much the same way for them until 1954, when Ghassan's father received notice that his land was to be expropriated to provide building space for Nazareth Illit.

In March 1953 the Acquisition of Land (Operations and Compensation) Law was promulgated to legitimize just such expropriations. The family and their neighbours were told that compensation money had been deposited in the bank for them, and would be paid as soon as they vacated their homes. Compensation at the time was usually between $40 and $50 a *dunum*, i.e. less than a third of what a *dunum* produced in one year!

Anyway, Ghassan's family had no wish to leave the land on which they had lived for generations. They refused to go. Builders arrived with lorries and bulldozers to start work on the new road which was to link Nazareth Illit with Tiberias on the Sea of Galilee. The road led through the Musmar land. Still the family stayed. They went to court, on the grounds that this particular piece of land provided the earth which they needed to keep the pottery going, and that their whole living would be threatened if it was taken away from them. A government representative raised the amount of compensation they were offering, but Ghassan's father refused it.

'Would it be so terrible if you built your houses on the land you have and we continued to live here?' he asked.

'Yes,' came the reply. 'This is Jewish land and Arabs are not allowed to live here.'

The construction workers started to level the land, their bulldozers flattening fruit trees and burying the fruit. Ghassan's father and brothers tried to chase them away and stopped them working whenever they could. One day seven coach-loads of workmen arrived to survey the land for a chocolate factory they wanted to build. The family started to throw stones to drive them away.

A Jewish woman approached them, saying in Arabic, 'This land does not belong to you.'

'But my father and grandfather lived and died here,' replied Ghassan's father.

A man came over and tried to calm them. Suddenly Ghassan's mother shot forward, and before anyone knew what she intended, she had taken the man's watch! 'Hey!' yelled the man. 'What do you think you're doing?'

'I'm taking your watch, it's mine now.'

'Oh no, it's not!'

'You see,' said Ghassan's mother, 'I only took your watch, and you're furious. And you want to take my home!'

Ghassan's sister started to take photographs. Someone must have called the police, who came with two big cars. By now a real fight was in progress. Ghassan's family was told to get into the cars to go to the police station. Ghassan's father insisted on changing his clothes and shaving before going into the town, but eventually he and his sons were ready to go with the police – only they refused to travel in the police cars, saying the people would think they were collaborators. All this time the sister was taking photos. One of the policemen, a man named Franco, asked her what she was doing.

'What do you want to do with those photos? Send them to Gamal Abdel Nasser?'

He made Ghassan's brother open the camera and destroy the film. Then he said, 'As you destroyed this film, so I will destroy your house.' The procession started towards the town and the Moscobiyeh – first a police car, then Ghassan's father with his sons on foot, then the second police car. A crowd lined the streets as far as Mary's Well.

At the Moscobiyeh father and brothers were interrogated and placed in cells, despite their protests. Meanwhile one of their employees (they had six workmen in the pottery) had notified their lawyer, who came and assured them that they need spend only an hour or so in the cells. He would get a court injunction to stop the work on the land. Father and brothers remained in the cells for about seven hours, and when they got home, a path for the road had been dug across their land. The trees were gone, the fruit buried in piles of earth.

The family went back to the court, but by now they had little hope of saving their home. So they asked to be given land rather than money in compensation for the land they were to lose. They received a plot of land on the other side of the new road, which now separates Nazareth Illit from Nazareth itself. In exchange for the 80 *dunums* of land they originally owned they received 15 *dunums* for a new house.

On this piece of land father and brothers hastily erected the house and brought their furniture bit by bit down the hill from the old house to the new. Even then they were not left in peace. An official who saw them carrying away their washbasin insisted that all the installations had been paid for with the house, and demanded that they pay for the washbasin. The family did receive some compensation for the trees, but they did not receive permission to dig a well on the new land, so were not able to plant new ones.

This family was among those who formed the *Al Ard* (The Land) group, an association which fought for the right of Arab Israelis to their land. A group of men, three from Nazareth, two from Haifa and two from Acre, met in Ghassan's father's house in April 1959. They were determined to speak out for the rights of the Palestinians in Israel and call for the Arabs to be united, since unity was their only strength. They approached others, especially in the Triangle area and among the university students, and started to publish pamphlets, each time under a different name, because they did not have permission to publish.

The pamphlets were printed on an ancient printing press, and as Mansour Kardosh, one of the original members from Nazareth, told me, it took a lot of muscle-power, because every time they were ready to go to press there was a power cut and they had to work the printing press by hand. People in Acre used to say to each other when the lights went out, 'Ah, the *Ard* people must be printing again!' Many nights were spent by candle-light. About half an hour after they were finished they usually found that the lights would come back on.

Pamphlets were distributed in Nazareth from hand to hand. They were free, but the people of the town would put a little money in the pockets of the distributors, and the group always covered the costs of printing. They were under constant pressure and often subject to house arrest, which meant they were not allowed to leave their own neighbourhoods, had to report to the police station every day at a certain time and be inside their houses from sunset to sunrise. Sometimes they were detained for periods varying from 48 hours to a month, always without charges being brought. Mansour Kardosh tells how he was once banished to Ard, a new town in the Negev, near the Dead Sea. 'I went there with 175 pounds in my pocket,' he reports, 'and I stayed in a hotel there, but I came back with 800 pounds. People gave us a lot of support, and not only in discussion.'

The group, which had grown considerably in the meantime, sent a memorandum to the Secretary General of the United Nations, Dag Hammarskjöld, copies of which were sent to all the foreign embassies in Israel, in which they complained about the land expropriation, the standard of education in the Arab sector and general discrimination. They were among the first Palestinians to digest the fact that Palestine was partitioned and the partition would have to be accepted. Strangely enough, they were subjected to a barrage of criticism in Israel for this acceptance of a *fait accompli*.

Israeli public opinion accused them of wanting to take parts of Israel: Galilee, the Triangle, Jaffa and the strip which includes Lydda and Ramleh, i.e. those parts of Israel which the partition plan allocated to the Palestinian homeland. Several members of the group, including Mansour Kardosh, Sabri Jeryis and Habib Qahwaji were arrested and accused of receiving money from Arab regimes. The Ard movement was outlawed. Sabri Jeryis and Habib Qahwaji were forced to go into exile, where Sabri Jeryis joined the PLO.[5] Some of the original members of Al Ard, such as Mansour Kardosh, are still active in socio-political projects in Israel today.

four *A prisoner in his own country*

They covet fields, and seize them;
houses, and take them away;
they oppress householder and house,
people and their inheritance.

(MICAH 2.2)

My father was coming home!

On 18 December 1958 the whole family went to meet him at the border crossing-point at Ras AnNaqoura (Rosh HaNikra in Hebrew) on the coast. While he recognized me immediately, my heart was saddened when he asked in a whisper who was the young lady who had just hugged him. He had not recognized Suad, his eldest daughter.

There was another disappointment – my brother Kamal came home with my father, but Rohi had decided to stay behind in Lebanon. He did not take Lebanese citizenship, but he did establish himself in business in Beirut and is now quite wealthy. Since the outbreak of the Lebanese civil war his wife and children have been living in Canada. Rohi commutes between Toronto and Beirut.

As a family we were never once all together at one time. My youngest brother, George, was born after Suad and I left Lebanon. My mother brought him and my sisters Rosette, Jeanette and Suheila home to Nazareth illegally in 1953. We do not have a single photograph of us all together. Now my father is dead we never shall.

But his return in 1958 prompted the type of celebrations which are only seen at a wedding feast. My father's return was the result of campaigning and great effort on the part of many people. In the course of his work he had often been in Lebanon prior to 1948. He had a visa to travel there and had never registered as a refugee, so we were able to argue that he had not fled the country but merely been away from home when the borders were closed. The fact that his wife and all but two of his children were officially residing in Israel also gave us good humanitarian grounds for seeking permission for my father to join us. My father and brother were two of the very few who were allowed to cross the Lebanese–Israeli border officially to return to their home.

Later I discovered that my brother and other relatives in Beirut had also worked hard to persuade my father to come home. He postponed leaving Beirut several times. In the end they gave him a huge farewell party, plied him with *arrack* and floated him over the border on a wave of emotion and alcohol.

At the time I did not really understand his hesitation. It seemed obvious to me that his place was with us, his family, but it proved difficult for my father to take up his life in Nazareth. He who had breakfasted in Beirut, lunched in Damascus and eaten supper in Amman had to queue for hours for a permit to leave Nazareth. He was afraid of the soldiers at the checkpoints. We'd had ten years to get used to them, but to my father, with stories of Israeli brutality heard from other refugees still ringing in his ears, they were terrifying. He said again and again that he felt as if he were in a large prison.

During the 1936–9 Arab uprising in Palestine my father had used his car to smuggle people and maybe other things between Nazareth and Damascus or Beirut under cover of his work. Several times he came under fire by the British Mandate forces. Once a British officer asked Dad to drive him from Nazareth to nearby Afula. On the way they picked up a Polish girl, a refugee from the Second World War. The officer made himself comfortable with her in the back seat and they started kissing passionately, a form of behaviour of which my father strongly disapproved. He put an end to it by braking sharply. In his own way he was more nationalistic than I was.

In the Arab countries in which he had lived and travelled, Nazareth and Galilee were still spoken of as occupied territories, which indeed they were. My father thought that he would come home to a place which was his own. The only difference would be the presence of soldiers. Even this was nothing new. He would have exchanged the British military presence for an Israeli military presence, just as he had already exchanged the Turkish imperial power for the British Mandate.

Dad never lost his belief that the Zionist regime would pass like the others. To his last breath (he died on the last day of 1986 and was buried on the first day of 1987) he never really settled in Israel, but he took the longer view. 'Go and read your history,' he used to say, 'time will not always be on the side of the Zionists. The Ottomans left and so did the British. Perhaps I will not see the change. Perhaps you won't. But your children may, and if not, their children will.'

In the meantime, the only news from the Arab countries came through the radio. Dad listened to the radio constantly. Cairo, Amman, Beirut, Damascus and the BBC – he listened to them all. However, he had no way of communicating with the son left alone in Beirut. He waited every year for Christmas, hoping to get a permit to visit his sister in Jerusalem for the holiday. She would be able to give him news of Rohi. Perhaps Rohi himself would come to Jerusalem. While in Lebanon my father had travelled regularly to Amman in Jordan. From there he would continue to Jerusalem, a matter of a 90-minute drive, and stay overnight at his sister's home. It would not have been difficult for Rohi to do the same.

Life in Nazareth was not the same as it had been under the Ottoman regime, or even during the British Mandate. Father had to contend with a new language and a new way of life. He was dependent on the goodwill of people he disliked. He often needed me to interpret for him on official business. He was dependent on me. In later years I added to his troubles through my political involvement. He often heard that he would receive certain rights or benefits only if he used his influence to curb my activities. 'Go and ask your son to help you,' the authorities would jeer, 'he thinks he's so clever!'

Dad found it humiliating to have to start all over again. It was difficult for him to find employment, so the obvious thing was for him to drive his own taxi, something he had done since he was a boy. The first step was to apply for an Israeli driving licence. The official at the office of vehicle registration explained that Dad would have to take a driving test. My father agreed – he said they could blindfold him and he would drive from Haifa to Tel Aviv! He made such an impression on the official that he issued the licence without further ado, but Dad felt the humiliation keenly.

With the help of the whole family we bought a suitable car. But then we had to license it as a taxi, and this proved an insurmountable obstacle. It was simply too expensive. Lacking an alternative, my father worked as a driver anyway, building up a circle of customers among friends and neighbours who could be relied upon to say that he was just doing them a favour if questioned by the police. The police were not always convinced and Dad was taken to court once or twice for driving a taxi without a licence. At one time his driving licence was taken away from him for six months, causing us great hardship.

There were people, including some in authority, who sympathized with him. Many of the ladies of the town were glad to have him drive them, knowing that they could trust him absolutely. But Dad stopped working early, angry and defeated. Often he wished he had stayed in Beirut. 'There I could accept that I was a refugee,' he said, 'but here I am treated like a refugee in my own country.'

At first I found it difficult to understand my father's dilemma. I accused him of ingratitude towards us for all our efforts to make his return possible.

'Riah,' he said, 'believe me, I do appreciate what you have done. But try to understand how hard it is for me. I feel as if I'm still in exile – in my own country, in my own home!' I began to observe things I had not noticed before. My sisters had grown used to seeing me as the authority in the family. They came to me for pocket money. When I told them to get on with their homework, they went and did it. When my Dad told them to do their homework, they hesitated and looked at me.

One day I came home to find Suad in tears because Dad had shouted at her. 'You have to obey your father,' I said.

'But I didn't do anything wrong,' she cried.

He started to shout at the other children, especially his daughters. My father was naturally a gentle man, but now he was desperate to regain his authority. I often went to bed in tears, needing him but feeling as if there was a barrier between us. I remembered how he used to play with us. In summer we spread our mattresses on the floor in the big hall, the coolest room in the house. There he used to wrestle with us, testing our strength. All of a sudden he could no longer play with us. He felt shy with us. Instead of being between Nazareth and Beirut the border had come into our home: it was between us.

I was earning my first wage by this time, and I would sneak into my parents' room and leave the unopened wage packet on their bedside table, trying to make it easier for them to accept that I was the breadwinner. Most Arab children brought their wages home to their parents, who were responsible for educating them, building a house for them or providing a dowry.

The money was used for the good of all the family, regardless of who was earning it. But my father, who had worked hard all his life, found it difficult to accept his dependence on me. Suddenly he was the father, but not a real father; the head of the household, but he had no authority; a homeowner but not in possession of his house; at home, but an outsider.

My brother Kamal was also finding it difficult to readjust. He was six years old when he left Nazareth and sixteen when he came back. We tried to persuade him to finish school, but he was ashamed because his English was poor (he learned French while in Lebanon) and he knew no Hebrew.

Many of us who had left school in 1948 or were too old to learn Hebrew at school have similar problems. In Nazareth and the surrounding areas we believed for a long time the Israeli occupation was temporary. Why should we learn Hebrew?

Jewish immigrants to the country are given six months' free, intensive tuition in the excellent Hebrew language schools called *ulpanim*. No such provision was made for Arab citizens of Israel. I taught myself by reading the Old Testament in Hebrew, but others never properly picked up the language. Reading and writing Hebrew is especially difficult for them, as Hebrew has its own script. This makes every official letter which arrives in the mail an alarming mystery, every visit to the tax office, the social welfare office or the pensions office an intimidating and humiliating experience. Many of our older people speak English if they leave their own neighbourhoods, hoping to pass for tourists rather than expose themselves as second-class citizens.

Kamal returned from Beirut a very rough young man. My father had often been away from home on business and left Rohi and Kamal to look after themselves. Being the younger, Kamal was expected to clean the house, bake the bread and do the shopping. Both Rohi and my father depended on Kamal because he was stronger than they were. Rohi was a slightly built person, like myself, but Kamal was bigger even than his father. With no feminine influence to soften him, Kamal developed sharp contours and hard edges. When he came to Nazareth he was continually fighting. If he caught a young man so much as glancing at my sisters he was ready to fight them.

He was also strict with my sisters. Like all the young girls they liked to sit in the big hall of our house with the door open and watch the world go by. Kamal forbade them to sit by the open door, until they complained to their father, who made it clear that he would decide what was fitting behaviour for his daughters.

Kamal started work in Tel Aviv as a labourer. He lived with other young people and mixed with Jews, mainly from the poorer community. On my return from India I discovered he had saved no money, although he had been working for four or five years. His wages were good, and we persuaded him to bring the money home so that we could build a house for him, which we did. We built it on the flat roof of my parents' home, in the traditional way. I was very grateful to use it when I brought my bride to Nazareth in 1967, only to find the vicarage still under repair and roofless! Strangely, Kamal changed completely once he married. Now he is soft-tempered and easy-going. He still amazes all of us.

Relations between my mother and father were also strained for a long time. Now that I am older I can imagine how difficult it must have been for them to take up their life together after a break of five years – a period which had been so difficult for both of them. They had little or no privacy. They were living in two rooms with seven children who were no longer small. It took them a long time to readjust.

Once, feeling my father's sadness, I suggested we go for a walk together. He took me into his confidence and I was shocked at what he told me. He asked me to intercede with my mother, to ask her to affirm his authority with the children. By then I had worked as a teacher and was already preparing for the ministry, but I had no experience in counselling – and here was my own father confiding in me.

This episode, painful as it was, stood me in good stead later, when I became involved with the Society of the Friends of the Prisoners, a group founded to give financial assistance for the rehabilitation of political prisoners. Financial help was not the only assistance prisoners and their families needed. More than once I was called on to comfort wives whose husbands were finding it difficult to readjust to family life after years of absence. Husbands who, while in prison, had depended on their wives to look after the home, cope with shortages and be mother and father to their children, suddenly became jealous and tyrannical when they came home, suspecting their wives of having relations with other men or of turning the children against their father. Sometimes a husband came to me in despair, feeling like a stranger in his own home, useless, unwanted, a failure.

I could not condone the actions of some of the men – those who had resorted to violence – but it is certainly true that even they had not acted out of greed or from selfish motives. According to their own horizons they were patriots. I hope that my own early experience with my father helped me to find the words to reassure them and give them strength to take up their broken lives.

At the time I knew only that I had usurped Dad's authority. On the one hand he was very proud of me, on the other he felt I was his rival.

five *Eggs for India*

In the summer after my graduation from high school in 1956 our Anglican priest, Reverend Khalil Jamal, married an English-woman and left us to go and live in England. I stood in front of the locked gates of Christ Church in Nazareth and a voice seemed to be saying 'Who will open these gates?' It was then that I knew I was called to the ministry.

I wrote to the Anglican Archbishop, Campbell MacInnes, in Jerusalem and he sent Canon Edward Avery, who later became a friend, to interview me. Canon Avery asked me why I wanted to become a priest. The interview was conducted in English, which made it difficult for me to express exactly what I meant. I thought that the Anglican community needed revitalizing, but what I actu-ally said was, 'I think our church needs a reformation'! This did not go down too well at all, but Canon Avery promised to see what he could do for me. After some discussion I was accepted as a candidate for the ministry and it was decided that I should study in India, at Bishop's College. I did not know much about India, but a college for bishops sounded an excellent choice!

Bishop's College

And so, on 25 August 1960, I arrived in New Delhi after a gruelling flight in a propeller machine. My first impression of India was un-deniably positive. Passengers to Calcutta were taken to the impos-ing Ambassador Hotel for the night, and as I relaxed and stretched, the tiredness of the journey fell away and India seemed a most inviting place. The next morning we continued to Calcutta, where reality hit me in the form of a wall of heat on leaving the plane. As a greeting, we were sprayed with DDT to keep off the insects. In Calcutta it was pouring with rain! In a crowded and not particularly clean bus we were driven from the airport to the so-called city terminal, and on the way I had my first chance to view the slums of Calcutta, on either side of the road. Wooden shacks seemed to be floating on the water.

My mood of optimism from the night before was rapidly wearing off, and took a further blow when the Principal of the college – who had been waiting to greet me – showed me to the guest room where I was to spend my first night. The door opened to reveal a dark, dank room containing a chair and a bed and dominated by a huge mosquito net, half black and half white, which immediately summoned half-buried associations of an India full of snakes and insects. The creaking of a fan which stirred the muggy air broke the silence. I had arrived.

During the first night I still believed I might refresh myself a little with a 'shower' – a bucket of water and a mug with which to pour it over oneself – but I soon found that after drying myself with a towel rapidly becoming as limp and damp as I felt, I was immediately bathed in sweat again. So I lay in bed, hardly able to breathe, and wondered just what had made me even consider coming to India.

Next morning in the refectory, I looked around at my fellow students. Apart from me, all were from the subcontinent, Indians, Pakistanis, Ceylonese and Burmese. In my innocence I set out to learn a little of the local language, only to discover that there were 16 official languages and as many as 532 dialects in India, and most seemed to be represented in the college. So English was the medium of communication for all of us. During the day I was given a timetable and introduced to what was to be my routine for nearly 365 days a year for the next three years.

Discipline was very strict. At 5.00 the rising bell rang, matins were at 5.30, at 6.00 we had meditation, 6.30 Holy Communion and then breakfast at 7.15. After breakfast, classes took us up to intercession at 11.45, then lunch and classes again from 2.00 till 4.00, after which we had compulsory physical exercises until 6.00, followed by evensong and dinner, after which we were 'free' to prepare the next day's studies, until 10 o'clock came and with it compline. After that we could lie down and try to sleep, an endeavour generally foiled by the suffocating humidity. My strong will came to my aid and, in spite of later sickness, I made good progress and got consistently high marks. The Principal even told me I should perhaps pay less attention to my lectures and more attention to the spiritual side of my training!

It quickly became apparent to me that this routine would leave little or no time for getting to know the country and its people. Even if I had had the money to do it, my timetable would have stopped me going out very much. I heard repeatedly 'You are here to train for the ministry, you must learn to discipline your body and your spirit, to live on the minimum.' I have since come to appreciate this training, it has stood me in good stead.

India seemed very strange to me, but strangest of all, and the thing I thought I would never get used to, was the food. This consisted of two pieces of bread in the morning, with just a smear of jam on them. They were washed down by tea with powdered milk. Very occasionally I had the money to buy an egg to complement this diet. The midday meal consisted of boiled rice with *dhal* (lentils) and a very hot, spicy sauce containing hardly any meat or protein. Egg curry, for example, contained half an egg per portion. In the evening we ate what was left over from the midday meal with chapati, the unleavened Indian bread. If you arrived 15 minutes late it was like trying to eat a stone.

Food was not provided by the college. We paid a student who paid the cook. Sometimes we paid extra to have an omelette. The cook would come and ask how many wanted to eat an omelette. The first time this happened we fell into the trap. 'Four,' we said. We got four omelettes – from one egg. This culinary experience even prompted us to make up a song: 'Sultan is a miracle-worker, he can make four omelettes from one egg.'

But I became sick. I lost a lot of weight and grew very weak. Suddenly my hair started falling out. In the morning I found handfuls of it all over my pillow, a frightening experience at the age of 24 – although I got used to it later. One night I became convinced that I was going to die. I wept like a child, I felt so weak. The Archbishop kept writing to tell me I had to see it through. I wrote to all my friends who were studying in other countries, begging them to help me find a place somewhere else, anywhere else, anywhere but here! I never told my parents I was unhappy, however, not wishing to worry them. Later I discovered that two other Palestinian priests (who later became bishops), Elia Khoury and Aql Aql, had been sent to India and Pakistan to study. One stayed for nine months, the other escaped after only two.

I developed recurring bouts of tonsillitis with high fever, which were completely debilitating. The humidity in Calcutta made it hard to resist illness. I was taken to hospital, but they hesitated to operate because I was so weak. They suggested I should go home.

As I left, the Principal said, 'I'm sure you will think fifteen times before you come back.'

'Fifteen times?' I replied, 'Fifteen times ten, sir.'

I made my way to Delhi, where I went to the post office to cable my parents that I was coming. On the way I had an experience which gave me a great shock. An old man with a long white beard and uncut hair held out to me a little typed note, blue print on a white card. I can picture it still. It said 'Try Your Luck.'

'Get off my back,' I said rudely, 'I know my luck.' I did not know this man, nor he me. We had never met before, no one in that entire huge city knew me. He said to me, 'You are leaving India now, but you will be back – sooner than you think.'

At Tel Aviv airport my parents were waiting for me. My father took one look at me and said, 'You're ill!'

I was determined never to go back to India, but a few days after my arrival, on my way to visit Revd Khalil Duaybis, who was then looking after the parish of Christ Church, I passed the Abu El-Assal taxi rank where a number of my uncles worked. One of them spotted me and called, 'Hey! Is it true that you failed your BA?' Of course, I took this as strong provocation and could not wait to get back to my studies, to prove him wrong. I tried every way I knew to get a place in another college, but without success. The Archbishop was adamant that this was the only way for me. It was India or nothing. I was the first to arrive back after the holidays.

This time things were different. My brother Rohi sent me money to improve my standard of living, and the expatriate staff (two English and one Canadian lecturer at Bishop's College) promised to give me one meal a day. I shared the expense with them. Thus I discovered that it was possible to live decently, even in Calcutta. This time I was determined to get out and meet people. We used to worship at the cathedral, where we were expected to sing. At the cathedral I met a Chinese family and became friends with one of the sons, Steve. They owned a shipyard and were well off. I was fascinated to learn that there were Chinese Christians. It became customary for Steve to take me to his home every Sunday after evening service. There we would enjoy a Chinese meal, which has left me with an abiding taste for Chinese food. Steve decided I needed to see more of the country and offered me the use of their spare Vespa, so I got myself a driving licence and India began to open up before me. My style of driving became famous in the neighbourhood and earned me the nickname of 'the pilot'.

Gradually I discovered that there was an international student community in Calcutta, and the students introduced me to people in office. In this way I came to know the Egyptian Consul-General and the Egyptian Trade Delegation, and through the Trade Delegation I found a way to help some of the poorer institutions. The Delegation dealt in tea and cotton, buying Indian tea and selling cotton from Egypt. They received thousands of kilograms of tea for testing, most of which was not needed. Until then, the rest was burned. I asked if I could have what was not needed, and we started taking it to orphanages, old-people's homes, and similar institutions. This helped me to meet another circle of people. I started speaking to groups about the situation in Israel and Palestine. The Egyptian Consul told me, 'I hope that Palestine will be liberated one day – and then I expect to meet you as her ambassador.'

I took part in the Indian Independence Day celebrations and national holidays. I did not gain weight, but my spiritual health improved greatly. At one point my passport had nearly expired, so I wrote to the Israeli Consul-General in Bombay and asked for a renewal. With the application forms he sent an interesting letter, saying that the government would be happy to offer me work when I returned to Israel, or they could offer me a good job if I would like to stay in India. At the time I thought little more about it.

In the summer of 1963 I decided to visit Bangalore. While there I visited the United Theological College, which I found very different to what I was used to. First of all the climate was much more pleasant, since United Theological College lies about 3,000 feet above sea level, in the Nilgris area. Then the atmosphere at the college was entirely different. I decided that I would like to continue my studies for another year.

United Theological College

At UTC the students were international and the college offered a very different vision of Christian living. People there were able to laugh and I learned that laughter can be part of a Christian way of life. Worship was optional, although I made it a point to attend morning prayer every day. Students were encouraged to take an interest in the outside world. My room-mate, another Steve, was from America. We both grew beards, became good friends and started living as I had imagined student life to be.

Apart from my activities with the international student association, I got to know and love a Syrian family. They owned a factory called the 'Egyptian Factory', which produced and sold sweets, cakes and Chiclets chewing gum. This family was known in Bangalore for its good works. When Gamal Abdel Nasser visited the city they were asked to prepare the food for him and also for the Iraqi President, Abdel Salam Arif. Passing the factory one day I noticed the name, and thinking the people must be Egyptian I went in and asked for *baclawa*, but in English. '*Ahlan waSahlan!*' cried the man behind the counter.

'Are you from Egypt?' I asked in Arabic.

'No, from Syria, from Damascus. And you?'

I told him, 'I am a Palestinian, from Nazareth, from Galilee. I live in Israel . . .'

He jumped up and started calling his six sons; 'Farouk, Mahmoud, Ossama . . . come and meet your new brother!'

One by one they came, and from the very first day I felt like one of the family. 'Come and eat with us,' they invited. 'I'm sure the food in college is not like ours.'

'What do you cook?' I asked.

'Our wives are Syrian, we cook Arab food.' After that day I never felt hungry again. Every time I felt I needed a little extra, something familiar, I went to my new family. They made me so welcome that I could almost feel able to go and raid their fridge. They helped me find my way around, introduced me to people and even gave me my first driving lessons in their car. Through them I met a group of Egyptian students who were in Bangalore studying aeronautics. I discovered that India had highly developed industries – the steel industry, the aviation industry. Up to now I had thought that all of India was poverty-stricken, but later I discovered that India traded extensively in diamonds, for example.

The Egyptians were happy to cultivate my acquaintance, because they had seen my Iranian girlfriend. She was also a student, a Parsee by the name of Zareen. Unfortunately neither of us gave them the attention they were hoping for, so they started spreading rumours that because I was blue-eyed and came from Israel I must be a Jew. They tried to convince my Syrian friends of this, and the father called me to ask what was going on. I explained that I thought they were offended because Zareen did not want to go out with them.

'I am a Palestinian,' I said. 'My brother is in Beirut, we are of the Abu El-Assal family.' I had already told him the story of my name, which originated in Damascus. My father had a business friend in Damascus, called Abu Riah, who had no children. He asked my father to call one of his sons for him. 'If I have sons,' declared my father, 'the eldest one will be called Riah,' and so I got my name. I am possibly the only Riah in Israel.

It was the holy month of *Ramadan* and I had promised to fast with the family. Muslims do not eat between sunrise and sunset during Ramadan. I joined them in the evening to break the fast. At the end of the month, the father invited me to join them for the feast of Eid Al Fitr, which closes the fast. He also invited the 17 Egyptian students. In the morning the father led the prayers for the Muslim community in Bangalore, then the meal was prepared. I was told to wait in the factory until all the guests were seated, then one of the sons said, 'Shall we eat now?' Everyone was hungry after the fast, but the father said, 'No, the guest of honour has not yet arrived, go and see if he is coming.'

As agreed, the young man slipped out of the room and came to fetch me. A place had been reserved near the father's place at the head of the table. He stood up and hugged me, kissing me on both cheeks. I greeted them all with the traditional greeting and shook hands with his sons. Before I could continue around the table, the father said, 'Wait!' He turned to the Egyptians. 'If there is an Arab among us, it is Riah,' he declared. 'I understand that you stopped talking to him. I want you to know that we know our people.' (In those days, people spoke of Greater Syria, which included Palestine.) With renewed confidence I continued shaking hands and we were reconciled, although my friendship with the Egyptians was never as warm as that with the Syrians.

I was now doing research on my thesis, which left me more time for myself. Since I was majoring in Islamics I was introduced to Dr Jai Singh, an authority on Islam, convert from Hinduism and eminent in the field of comparative religion. Dr Singh has written extensively for the *Encyclopaedia Britannica*. He helped me work out my thesis, a comparative study of Christian and Muslim mysticism, which involved visits to different places in the country.

I was given help to plan visits to both the Muslim community and to Christian ashrams (the Indian name for a monastery or convent). These took me to Kerala, Bihar, New Delhi and Bombay – where I discovered how small the world is.

It was Christmas and I was staying at the YWCA. Visiting one of the islands offshore I was waiting my turn for the ferry and looking at wares displayed on the pavement beside me, when I came face to face with two people who looked like Europeans. I looked at them idly, then looked again at the girl, who was staring back at me. 'Yes or no?' she asked.

'Yes,' I replied, 'You must be Helen.'

'And you are Riah.'

Helen was a Swiss girl who had worked as a nurse at the Nazareth Hospital five or six years earlier, and here we were standing next to each other in a street in Bombay, a city of millions.

Although I regretted my first year in India, I never regretted going back. In Bishop's College I had been given a solid grounding in the Old and New Testament. At UTC I learned not only about the Christian way of life, but also about Buddhists and Hindus. I lived in an interdenominational, international community and became involved in world affairs. I was active in the international student association, where we would organize meetings on Palestinian rights and on the rights of Black South Africans.

When I went to the station in Bangalore to start my journey home, there were perhaps fifty or a hundred people there to see me off – Indians, Anglo-Indians, Arab-Indians, Christians, Muslims and Hindus, boys and girls. As we hugged and said goodbye I told them I thought I must have been an Indian in my previous life, so much had I grown to love the country. The experience of India shaped my life and greatly influenced my decision to become involved in social and even political issues.

Back in Israel

Some time after I arrived home, I was invited to dinner by a relative. Various other people were there, including one man who was a stranger to me. We were introduced, but I did not catch his name. I noticed that he did not look Arab. I thought he must be a business acquaintance of my relative. This man took a great interest in my experiences in India, asking me about my life there, my financial situation, my contacts. Laughing about how hard life had been at times, I told the company the story of the omelettes and how hard it was to get eggs in India.

After the meal this man offered me a lift home. It was quite a long way to my parents' house, so I accepted gratefully. As we were driving along he asked me whether I would like to go back to India.

'I don't understand,' I said.

'I could offer you a job there,' replied the man.

'I have a job,' I replied. 'In fact I have more than a job, I have a calling. I went to India to prepare myself for my ministry, and now I have returned home to take it up, as I believe God wants me to do.'

'I understand your church people are not making it easy for you,' he said.

This was true, but I wondered that this stranger knew about such internal church discussions – especially since he was obviously not a Christian, not to mention an Anglican Christian. Becoming very curious, I feigned interest. 'What kind of job are you thinking of?' I enquired.

'Certainly it would be a different life than you had before,' he replied. 'I am talking about a good position and a lot of money. You would be in charge of a sort of trade delegation.'

I had told him of my contacts with the Egyptian trade delegation.

'If you could sell one egg a year to every Indian, we would be supplying India with four to five million eggs a year. This has absolutely nothing to do with politics,' he added.

I was not so sure. 'Please would you stop the car here,' I asked. 'I think I would prefer to walk the rest of the way.'

'You'll regret it,' he said.

'Maybe,' I said, 'but I think you've been talking to the wrong person.'

Later I discovered that he was working for the Shin Beth in Nazareth (in Nazareth nothing can be kept secret for long), and that it was his job to interview students who returned from their studies abroad.

six *An urgent engagement*

Life in Israel, 1964–

By the time I returned from India I had changed a lot. During the 1950s I had been mainly busy trying to support my family, and my concerns were mostly more of a personal nature, although I did march in demonstrations on Labour Day. India changed all that. I learned that there was much going on in the world. I became interested in the Indians' struggle for independence and studied the teachings of the great Mahatma Gandhi and the life of Jawaharlal Nehru. Through my activities in the international students' union I had met people from South Africa, Latin America, Korea and Vietnam, among others. It was a period of change and unrest in the world.

I arrived home ready to serve and eager to begin the work of revitalizing the Church. I was young and enthusiastic, full of new ideas; and of course I upset a lot of people. I was looked on as a revolutionary, a rebel out to provoke my more established colleagues, and they resented me. Perhaps I found it difficult to accept authority because I had been head of a household from such a young age, maybe I was affected by the general atmosphere of the Sixties. In any case I found it impossible to remain silent when I perceived injustice, whether towards me or anybody else.

While I was still in my twenties I was ordained deacon and put in charge of the parishes of Haifa and Shefa'amr. Many of my older parishioners found it difficult to relate to me. Fresh out of college, I took great care writing my sermons, explaining theological questions with the aid of the big words I had learned. I believed the congregation was happy with my preaching, until one day an old man of Shefa'amr, Amin Farah, invited me to lunch with him. Although in his seventies, Amin was a very faithful member of the church, always there to ring the bells and dust the pews. After lunch he said to me, 'Riah, I want you to lower the basket a bit.'

'What basket?' I asked, mystified.

So he told me how, in older times, the food in a house was kept in a basket which was suspended from the ring set in the keystone of the ceiling and lowered by means of a pulley construction. When the children wanted to eat, mother or father would lower the basket so they could reach it. I got the message. It seems to be one of my weaknesses to aim too high.

It was brought home to me that I was resented when a friend called me one day and, laughing, recounted the trouble he had had getting hold of me. My friend had asked for 'Priest Riah'.

'We have no priest called Riah here,' a man replied.

Somewhat irritated, my friend said, 'Aren't you from Nazareth? I want to speak to Riah Abu El-Assal.'

'Oh, you want to speak to *Deacon* Riah!' he said.

Though I was not popular with my superiors or with all of my parish, there was one group of parishioners I was very popular with – those with daughters of marriageable age. I was reminded of a joke I had heard in India: A young priest was sent to a hill station to take up his first assignment. After a while, his bishop received a worried letter. The attentions of a certain young lady of the parish were becoming so obvious it was embarrassing. Perhaps he should seek a transfer? The bishop wrote back a reassuring letter saying that this was a normal development and he would learn to cope with it. The young priest replied with an urgent appeal for advice – now there were several girls chasing him. The bishop cabled succinctly: 'Safety in numbers!' The reply cable came: 'Exodus comes before Numbers. Leaving.'

I found a different solution. Since my bachelor state was the main problem, the obvious answer was to marry. So I did. When I was teaching at St John's school in Haifa in 1958, Suad, her twin sister Najat and her brother Toufiq had been my students, so they were well known to me personally, although I had never looked on Suad as a potential bride. Certainly I had noticed that she and her sister were very good-looking girls, but mostly I remembered that they were naughty. Being good-looking they were spoiled by many of the teachers – but not by me.

As a teacher I visited their home and spoke to their father. Sadeq Abboud was very supportive of the school. Indeed, he was a very good man and widely respected, not only in his own community. He was greatly mourned when he died in 1963.

When I decided to ask for Suad's hand, I asked my mother and father to come with me to visit her family, together with the priests who were my colleagues, as is the tradition in our society. A little later we became engaged.

My brother Kamal met and became engaged to Najat. We decided to make it a double wedding, and were married on 1 April 1967, my 30th birthday. Shortly after our wedding, I was asked to transfer to the parish of Christ Church, Nazareth. I had learned from my experience in Haifa and resolved to approach my new ministry in Nazareth differently. Nazareth was (and is) the biggest Anglican parish in Israel and I felt honoured to be entrusted with its care. I was determined to prove worthy of this trust.

From the beginning, Suad and I kept an open house. Although we still had not been married long, we seldom enjoyed a leisurely cup of morning coffee in our pyjamas, but had to be ready to receive the first visitors by seven o'clock. The older people especially, having nothing to do themselves and nowhere to go to meet others, came to our home to sit and chat and drink coffee. The vicarage was the upper storey of a beautiful house situated at the edge of the old Latin Quarter of Nazareth, at the entrance to the *suq* and across the way from the church. This house was built by the governor of Nazareth District in Ottoman times and is graced by a large balcony running the length of its front and overlooking the town and the hills opposite. Here we could sit in the evenings and watch the full moon rise over the hills behind the newly completed Roman Catholic Church of the Annunciation. We also watched, with less enthusiasm, the houses of the Jewish new town of Nazareth Illit rise on the same horizon.

In a cupboard in the vicarage I had found the parish files and made it my job to go through them all. They had been locked up in the cupboard for so long they were becoming musty. I found important documents and trivia, all mixed up and piled on the shelves anyhow. There were certificates of baptism, marriage and death. There were wills and titles of church property and lists of the names of members of the parish. All needed to be viewed, sorted and filed away properly. I spent two whole months on this work, in air thick with dust – and I have suffered from an allergy ever since.

As a priest in the Middle East you are not only pastor, but also landlord and judge. In Israel there is no secular family law. All citizens must be registered as a member of one religious community or another, and notice of membership sent to the Ministry of Religious Affairs. There is no civil marriage or divorce in the country. Thus, as a priest, I am also a judge of the Ecclesiastical Court in Nazareth and have to decide in conflicts concerning inheritance and, more importantly, in marital conflicts.

In the Anglican Church divorce is not allowed, but provisions are made for official separation in the event that a marriage breaks down irreparably. The priest will make every effort to reconcile the conflicting sides, by counselling and giving spiritual guidance, but if he is not successful, he will meet the parties again in court. There are a minimum of three judges at every court session, a team usually composed of priests and lawyers. Sessions are held as often as necessary, which sometimes means every three weeks. Each party is given a hearing, at which minutes are taken, then the judges decide the issue in accordance with their findings and ecclesiastical rulings. The division of property is dealt with and financial provision made for the wife and children.

But as a priest you are not only called on to regulate the end of a marriage – you are also involved at the beginning of it. One morning at 5.45, in my early days in Nazareth, I was woken by the urgent ringing of the doorbell. It was winter, the weather was cold and wet and it seemed obvious to me that only a calamity such as a sudden death could have brought someone to call on me at such an hour. Fearing the worst, I opened the door. Standing on the doorstep was a bedraggled parishioner, an elderly widower in his sixties.

'Come in, come in, whatever is the matter, what's happened?' I said.

'I've come to ask you to officiate at my engagement,' he answered.

'Good Lord, it's quarter to six in the morning', I said. 'You frightened the life out of me.'

'Sorry, I thought I might miss you if I came later,' he replied.

An engagement is an important ceremony in our traditional society. In spite of the fact that many of our young people study, most of them continue to live at home until they marry. When a young man wishes to marry, he consults with his parents, his brothers and sisters, aunts and uncles and other relatives, and together they will try to find a suitable girl for him. Various suggestions are made, and when the young man and the family are happy with a choice, the parents approach the parents of the girl. If her parents signal a positive interest, the elders of the boy's family invite their priest to go with them to visit the girl's family. There, they officially ask for her hand. Her father consults with the girl and her mother, and probably other members of the family, and if they decide that the young man might make a suitable husband, they agree. The young man and the girl are given a short time to get to know each other, then the engagement is celebrated officially. The priest extols the boy's behaviour and character. He formally asks again for the girl's hand on behalf of the boy's family, the parents say '*mabruk*', giving their blessing to the engagement, then the priest reads a passage from the New Testament, usually the passage in praise of love from 1 Corinthians 13, and the engagement is sealed.

The real fun starts if one of the two wants to break off the engagement. It is customary for the young man to present his fiancée with valuable gifts of gold, clothing, delicate linen and the like on their engagement. When he visits his fiancée, which he is expected to do daily, or at least as often as possible, he brings more little gifts. Sometimes they go out together, maybe even to the cinema, always accompanied by a chaperon – the young lady's mother, brother or sister – of course. If the boy decides to break off the engagement, his fiancée keeps all the gifts. If she comes to the conclusion that he is not the right husband for her, she and her family have to return everything. As you can imagine, this procedure can become very acrimonious.

Some young men even present a claim for the ice-cream they bought at the cinema, not to mention the price of the tickets.

The poor priest has to arbitrate between them and try to bring the episode to an elegant close with no loss of face on either side. This can be costly not only with regard to time, but also with regard to his nerves. For this reason alone I am always genuinely glad to see the young couples in my flock happily married! I still have nightmares about the time a young man came to me on the eve of his wedding, and told me he wanted to call the whole thing off. It fell to me to announce the cancellation in church the next morning (it was to have been a Sunday wedding) and I sincerely hope I never have to go through such an ordeal again.

seven *High tea*

Two men were seated opposite each other in a train carriage,
speeding through the English countryside. One stared fascinated at
the turban of the other, and asked, 'Excuse me, but why have you
got that cloth wrapped around your head?'

'I am Sikh,' replied the other.

'But if you're sick, shouldn't you see a doctor?'

'No, no, you don't understand. I am Sikh of religion!'

'Ah, yes, I'm sick of religion, too!'

Anglicans in Israel

So you may ask why I decided to become a priest of the Anglican
Church, a tiny minority community in the Holy Land. What is
more it is a church looked upon as alien by many local Christians.

The Anglican girls' orphanage in town did indeed fly the Union
Flag and celebrate the official birthday of King George with a
picnic outing; and we prayed for the British royal family in our
church services. English had become the language of general use
in the Cathedral Close, even when two Palestinians were talking
together. The influence of the expatriate church hierarchy also
led to more bizarre customs, such as that adopted by some of our
community of taking tea at four o'clock – Greenwich Mean Time!

In the 1940s, when I was a boy in Nazareth, Anglicans were
viewed with mistrust among Palestinians. Some suspected us of
having special relations with the British Mandate powers. We did
not enjoy a privileged status. The Mandate government even

refused to recognize us as a religious community under the Ottoman *millet* system. We had to wait for recognition from the Israeli government in 1970. We are still waiting for tax exemption, which is granted to the Roman Catholic Church. Tax exemption would mean that medical and educational materials and equipment badly needed by our hospitals and schools could be imported duty-free.

I am proud to be an Anglican – or Episcopalian as we call ourselves now. I am proud of our reputation for honesty and integrity, and of the role we have played in our society. I value the tradition of discipline introduced by the missionaries of the German Protestant church, which for a time was closely allied to our own.

But there have been times when I found it hard to belong to such a Western church in our oriental society. There were times when I saw it as another burden; just another dimension of my conflict of identities. A minority within a minority within a minority – how minor can one get?

And yet many Anglicans, far more than their numbers would suggest, have become prominent figures in Palestinian society and leaders of our people. There are fewer than a thousand Anglicans in Israel – men, women and children – yet there have been two Anglican members of the Knesset, one representing the Mapam Party and one, my wife's uncle Emile Habiby, representing the Communist Party. Emile is also a celebrated writer who won the Israel Prize for Arab Literature. His works have been translated into many languages. Outside Israel we can look up to Hanan Ashrawi, one of the best-known spokespersons for the Palestinians in the Middle East peace process – and an Anglican.

Musa Nasser, who founded the West Bank university of Bir Zeit in his own home and built it up to be the foremost Palestinian university, was an Anglican. There is an Anglican, Bishop Elia Khoury, on the Executive Committee of the Palestine Liberation Organization and an Anglican, Ibrahim Souss, is the Palestinian diplomatic representative to France. The former Palestinian representative to the Netherlands, my friend the late Ghazi Khoury, whom we will meet again, was an Anglican. The Anglican influence has also extended to many others, Christian and Muslim Palestinians, who were educated in our schools.

Our own Christ Church School was the first school in Nazareth. It opened in October 1851, 20 years before the church was dedicated. The Protestant tradition of education encouraged discussion and debate, which were taboo in other traditions. We were taught in Arabic and English, and our study centred very much on the Bible, which we were encouraged to read. While we were given Bibles as confirmation presents and learned verses from it by heart, other denominations discouraged their lay members from reading the Holy Scriptures, which were often read in Greek or Latin, languages the ordinary people did not understand. Thus we were better equipped for dialogue and learned to be independent in our thinking. This has prepared us not only for leadership, but also to be bridges of understanding in the conflict in which we find ourselves.

Originally, the Anglican Bishopric in Jerusalem was known as the Protestant Bishopric. It was established in 1841 in cooperation with the King of Prussia, who envisaged a world-wide Protestant union, with Jerusalem as its centre. The first aim of the Bishopric was to bring Christianity to the Jews of Palestine. In keeping with this goal the first bishop, Bishop Michael Solomon Alexander, was a former Jewish rabbi who had converted to Christianity.

The second bishop, Bishop Gobat, was a Swiss Protestant. He turned his attention towards the local Christians and ordained three Arab Protestant (Anglican) priests. The first, Michael Kamar, was ordained at Christ Church, on the day the church was consecrated, 1 October 1871. However, the Anglo-Prussian cooperation was short-lived. The Germans were dissatisfied with several aspects of it, in particular the British insistence that German-nominated bishops be reordained by the Anglican Church. In 1882 the agreement was annulled and the bishopric reconstituted as an Anglican bishopric in 1887.

Working together with the London-based Church Missionary Society (CMS), Bishop Gobat was responsible for the establishment of many schools in the Holy Land. His efforts were not wholly appreciated by the established churches of the region, who feared he intended to proselytize among their members. Bishop Gobat's activities spurred the Roman Catholic Church to reinstitute the Latin Patriarchate in 1847. When he opened a school in Nablus, the Greek Orthodox Church there read an excommunication against all those who sent their children to it.

The first half of the twentieth century saw many historic changes in the diocese. The Ottoman Empire broke up, and the Kingdom of Jordan and the republics of Lebanon and Syria were established. These were the years of the 'Arab Awakening', the desire for independence in the Arab peoples and a growing national movement. It was supported by the imperial powers of the time, France and Britain, who saw it as a useful weapon in their rivalry with the Ottoman Empire.

Perhaps it was the spirit of protest in the Protestant church which attracted Arab Christians in the early years of the century, at a time when the very first stirrings of the Awakening began to be felt. Along with Ottoman domination and the *millet* system there was a readiness among young people to cast off traditional authorities, including religious authority.

The Protestants played a crucial role in the Arab Awakening, again mainly through education. American Protestant missionaries built the American University in Beirut and started schools, including the first Arab girls' school in the Lebanon. Another important innovation was a printing press for printing textbooks in the Arabic language. The role of Arab Protestant Christians in the revival of Arab culture cannot be overestimated. I have always felt very much a part of this tradition, called upon to keep it alive and continue the ministry of education and enlightenment which it represents.

In Jerusalem, 1905 saw a first step taken towards the indigenization of the church with the formation of the Palestine Native Church Council. Local clergy and laity united together under the guidance of the Church Missionary Society to establish a self-governing, self-supporting system. The CMS was motivated by the hope that local Christians would be more successful than foreigners in winning Muslims to Christ.

But then came what we know in Arabic as *Al Nakba*, 'the catastrophe' – the expulsion of the Palestinians from their land by the victorious Zionist forces and the death of their dream of independence. As a result the Diocese of Jerusalem was divided. The Anglican communities which remained in Israel were isolated from those in Jerusalem and the rest of the Middle East. The Anglican Church in the neighbouring Arab countries faced the massive task of coping with the refugees and persons displaced by the war.

In this period of general disarray, the church provided much-needed leadership and humanitarian help, not only to its own members but to all those affected by the upheaval, Christians and Muslims alike, although it must be admitted that not all the leadership in the early years after the division of the diocese was so positive. In the south of Israel, Nichola Saba, elected vice-chairman of the Church Council, tried at the instigation of the District Commissioner to persuade the local Anglicans to sell their possessions and those of their church and emigrate to Brazil!

In 1957 a delegation of Anglicans from Palestine went to the Archbishop of Canterbury to ask him to consider making one of their own Bishop in Jerusalem. Their wish was not granted, but it was decided to install Campbell MacInnes as Archbishop in Jerusalem, and appoint Najeeb Quba'in as bishop of a new diocese of Jordan, Lebanon and Syria. When the Revd Jamal left for England and the Revd Musa Azar went to Jordan in 1956, only the Revd Rafiq Farah was left to care for the flock in Israel until the Diocese of Jordan, Lebanon and Syria sent the Revd Khalil Duaybis to help him in 1958.

Archbishop George Appleton, who succeeded Archbishop MacInnes in 1969, proposed installing a second bishop in Israel. However, I realized that this would mean a further division in the Anglican community of the Middle East. We would be a tiny minority, cut off from the affairs of the Church in the region, and I was one of those who fought the proposal. The Anglican Communion, meeting in Dublin in 1973, eventually decided to reunite the diocese, and in 1976 the Diocese of Jerusalem was created, which now comprises the Holy City, Israel, Jordan, Lebanon, Syria and the Occupied Territories of Palestine.

It was agreed that the next bishop of the diocese should be elected from among the local clergy, rather than an expatriate. Faiq Haddad became Bishop in Jerusalem and Aql Aql Assistant Bishop in Amman. The diocese is still run according to the Anglican tradition, with the bishop at its head, a House of Clergy and a

House of Laity which represents the 28 different congregations, six of which are still primarily English-speaking.

When I was elected Chairman of the Church Council in 1971 I decided to dedicate myself to the improvement of the administration of church property. Until I took over, the property was administered by a lawyer who charged 33 per cent of the income as his fee. I learned how to administer it myself. A lot of the church property in the Jaffa/Tel Aviv area was old and needed renovating. I made it my business to inspect all the property to see for myself what really needed to be done, and I searched for firms or craftsmen who would carry out the work for a reasonable price. I tried to employ people from Nazareth or Nazarenes who had moved to the area, believing that they would feel more loyalty towards the church.

It was not always easy to discover who the tenant was. Many houses had been taken over by Jewish families after 1948 and they were not registered in the church records. During this period I learned a lot about the problems of the Jewish sector of our society. Most, if not all, of the tenants of church property in the Jaffa and Tel Aviv areas were Jews, as were about 80 per cent of the Haifa tenants. But in Tel Aviv our property lay in a poverty-stricken area. I became aware of the misery of the Oriental Jews, those who had come to Israel from the Arab countries. Some of these tenants were small-time drug dealers. Others supported their families by fishing, but they were hounded by the authorities because they usually did not have a licence and were in competition with established fisheries. Few of their children attended school regularly.

Some tenants were very difficult to deal with. They thought that they could exploit the church's humanitarian principles. One tenant, a Jew from Morocco, threatened to kill me when I insisted he pull down an extension he had started building without permission. 'If I lose one penny over this,' he shouted, 'you lose your life!'

And to underline his statement he went into his room and brought out his Uzi submachine gun, which most Israelis carry when they are on reserve duty. Twice I was threatened by guns by drug addicts or pimps who had occupied church property in Jaffa and in the Tel Aviv area. However, once they had understood that in spite of my clerical collar I was not going to be played with, my relationship with these tenants usually became a good one. They appreciated the fact that I was willing to enter their homes, sit with them and accept a cup of tea. Sometimes I was even offered a glass of wine. These people taught me a lot, especially about their view of the *Ashkenazi* Jews (those from Europe and the United States). There were similarities in our situations which helped me establish a relationship of trust, which in turn made administration of the property much easier.

When they saw that the church was caring for its property and administering it for the benefit of the community, several people left us property in trust, either on their death or when they emigrated. In this way we have been able to increase the amount of land we own. Eventually the church property brought in enough money for the priests, teachers and other staff to receive regular stipends.

eight *For God's sake*

And God took Moses up on to a high mountain, and the countries of the world were spread before him, and God asked Moses: Which of these lands shall I give thee for thy people? And Moses (whose speech was not fluent) answered: Ca ... ca ... ca ... OK, said God, Canaan it is.

    Actually, Moses was looking at Canada.

Living faith

Not only is the role of the priest within his community significantly different in the Middle East, the whole question of faith has a completely different quality. Nowhere is this more true than in the Holy Land itself. Let me illustrate what I mean. In 1958 I was in Marseilles, where I worked in a World Council of Churches work camp for young people from all over the world. There I found myself working next to a young Jew from Morocco or Algeria, a young man of about the same age as myself. This boy told me that he was on his way to Israel with his family. I asked him what made him want to go to Israel, in particular.

'It's our Promised Land,' he replied.

I did not comment, but some time later we were digging a drainage ditch and, the sun being hot, had taken our shirts off to work. He noticed the cross around my neck.

'You're not Jewish?' he asked.

'No, I'm a Christian.'

'You mean to tell me you really believe in all that religious stuff?'

'Yes. Why, don't you?'

'No. If I jump off a high building, I die. If you fall in the sea, you drown. Where is God in all that?'

I was dumbfounded. 'How do you dare say such a thing,' I asked, 'when you just told me you are going to the Promised Land? You believe in the Promise, but not in the One who made it?'

I am often confused by the attitude of Jews to God and have come to the conclusion that many are confused in their own minds and some even misuse his name on purpose to justify their presence in the land. They have made God into a real-estate agent, but the Gospel says: 'God is spirit, and those who worship him must worship in spirit and in truth'! (John 4.24.)

Zionism started as a secular movement, and many of its first supporters were communists, as I have already mentioned. Its goal was to provide Jews all over the world with protection in the form of a homeland, and the first Zionists who came to Palestine were motivated by socialist rather than religious ideals. However, the establishment of the Jewish State is increasingly seen as a fulfilment of prophecy, a renewal of the covenant between God and his Chosen People, giving them an exclusive right not only to dwell in the land, but to take it by force as did Joshua and the kings of Israel, killing or expelling those aleady living here or making them 'hewers of wood and drawers of water'.

Like most Christians, I suppose, I had always thought of the biblical Israel not so much as the country of a certain tribe – the Jews or the Israelites – but as a symbol of God's covenant with his people and his care for them. As a child, like most Christian boys I expect, I identified with David in the Old Testament. I loved hearing from my grandmother the story of the simple shepherd boy who won a great victory against the giant warrior Goliath, and became king.

Recently I heard the story of a journalist who was visiting the West Bank when he witnessed a small boy masked with a keffiyah, throwing stones at Israeli soldiers. Fearing that the armed soldiers might harm the boy, he ran after him.

'What are you doing here, throwing stones?' the journalist asked. 'You should be at school.'

'What school?' the boy replied. 'The schools have been closed for months!'

'Well, go home and help your mum. I bet she doesn't know you're out here throwing stones. You didn't learn that from your parents.'

'No,' said the boy, 'I learned it at Sunday School. I learned it from King David.'

'And if you hit a soldier, would you do what David did? Would you cut off the soldier's head?'

'No, I would help him up and ask him to help me build a home from these stones, where we can both live in peace.'

The Israelis took the image of David's victory over Goliath to illustrate their fight against the Arab multitudes, and with it they took part of my childhood. Suddenly I was the Philistine of the Old Testament (the words Philistine and Palestine have the same root). In one sense I find this comforting. It at least proves that my claim to this land is at least as old as the Jewish claim. At the time my world fell apart. Suddenly I could no longer relate to the Old Testament. Was I to understand that I was the enemy of God's Chosen People? Suddenly, to sing the psalms calling on God to strengthen Israel was to pray for him to strengthen my enemy. When I prayed to the Lord of Hosts, I was praying to the God of the Israeli army (the Hebrew term for 'hosts' – *sabaoth* – is the ancient form of the modern Hebrew word *tzavuot* – armed forces[1]).

However I trace my history, it is bound up with this land which we continue to call holy. As a Christian I look to the Old and New Testaments for the origins of my faith. As an Arab I can trace my presence in the land at least to AD 33 and the Arabs present at the first Pentecost (Acts 2.11). Muslim and Christian Arabs look on themselves as heirs to the original covenant through Abraham's firstborn son Ishmael, who is looked on as the forefather of all the Arabs (which is why we refer to the Jews as our cousins). As a Palestinian I look for my ancestors among the Philistines.

So you see, for both Jews and Palestinians, the Bible is not only our spiritual guide, but a record of our history and proof of our roots in the land. We have always lived side by side. How can my presence here now suddenly stand in the way of the fulfilment of the Scriptures? And as a Palestinian Christian am I not also an heir to the Covenant through Jesus Christ, my Saviour? Is there really no room for me here?

I am very unhappy about the growing misuse of religion to erect barriers between communities, whether it is in the former Yugoslavia, in Armenia and Azerbaijan, or in India. It makes me very angry when a dictator like Saddam Hussein, who was a staunch atheist as long as he received support from the Soviet Union, looks to fool simple folk by writing *Allahu Akbar* on his flag and telling them that his war with the West is not about the control of the oilfields but a holy war against the Infidel. Similarly I abhor the cynical way in which the Israeli government with its secular Zionist history now exploits the Jewish religion and the Bible to 'prove' their claim to the Holy Land.

But it makes me most angry when I see how the different Christian denominations fight among themselves. Unfortunately, becoming a minority in Israel has not stopped this rivalry. For many years intermarriage between the different Christian denominations was almost unknown in Nazareth. I remember a story told me by a Maronite neighbour whose sister wanted to marry a Protestant boy. Their father went to the Maronite priest to tell him.

'Ah,' sighed the priest, 'I wish you had come to tell me of her death. I wish you had told me she wants to marry a Muslim. It would be better for her!' The marriage did not take place.

A joke which was popular in Nazareth told of three young ladies who presented themselves at a Roman Catholic convent and asked to be accepted as novices. The Reverend Mother asked the first girl what she had been previously.

'I was a teacher, Reverend Mother, but I wish to dedicate my life entirely to God.'

'If you are sure, enter and welcome!'

The second young lady had been a nurse, but wished to retire from the world. She too was made welcome.

When asked the same question, the third young lady blushed and stammered: 'I was a p ... p ... prostitute.'

The Reverend Mother fainted. A little cold water brought her round, whereupon she stared at the unhappy girl. 'What did she say?' the abbess asked, not wanting to believe her ears.

'She says she was a prostitute, Reverend Mother,' replied one of the nuns.

'Oh, thank goodness for that. I thought she said "Protestant"!'

Formerly the people of Nazareth lived close to their own church, which was a social centre as well as a place of worship. The town is informally divided into districts known as *haras*. Some *haras* are named for the families who live in them, but there are also the Greek Orthodox *hara*, the Roman Catholic *hara* (also known as the Latin Quarter) and the Maronite *hara*. The area of town originally inhabited by the Muslims is known as the *hara as-sharqiyya*, or Eastern Quarter. Our own Anglican church is built on the edge of the Latin Quarter, and according to one historian[2] for many years the Roman Catholics averted their eyes when they passed it.

Few people in the world are aware that in the land of the Holy One we celebrate three Christmases. The first, on 25 December, is celebrated by the Western churches (including the Roman Catholics, Greek Catholics, Maronites and Protestant churches); the second, on 7 January, by the Eastern churches (the Greek Orthodox, Coptic and Syrian churches); and the third, by the Armenians, on 18 January. We celebrate only two Easters.

In an era when weeping and demonstrations of grief were the order of the day on Good Friday, a father once took his son to the service at the Roman Catholic church. The boy asked his father why the people were crying.

'They are weeping because Jesus was crucified.'

'But Dad, who did it?'

'The Romans did it, because the Jews asked them to. The Jews and the Romans were responsible. Damn the Romans!'

'Damn the Jews!' cried the boy.

Two days later he went to the Easter service and was overjoyed to hear that Jesus was risen from the grave. At the end of the week his parents took him to the Greek Orthodox church for the Good Friday service there. Again the people wept and wailed.

'Dad, Dad – do you mean to tell me the Jews and the Romans have done it again?' cried the boy in alarm.

'No, no,' his father reassured him, 'this time it is the Greek Orthodox...'

Hundreds of appeals have been made by the laity to the church hierarchies, the bishops, archbishops and patriarchs, to demonstrate Christian unity by celebrating Easter together. After all, we have only one Bridegroom, why hold two weddings?

I sometimes ask myself – if a Muslim did want to convert, to whom would he turn? To the Greek Orthodox Church? The Greek Catholic Church? The Roman Catholic Church? The Anglicans? The Baptists? The Brethren? The Church of the Nazarene? The Church of Christ? The Church of God? The Seventh Day Adventists...? They are all represented in Nazareth alone. All claim to have the answer.

When I was young, the majority of the population of Nazareth was Christian. As children we drank from Mary's Well, and the water was holy to us. We prayed in the grottoes of the Roman Catholic and the Greek Catholic churches, where Jesus is believed to have lived and prayed.

Prayer was an integral part of our lives wherever we were; at work, at school, out swimming. My father, although he did not go to church, never left the house without a prayer. To this day my mother crosses herself every time she gets into a car. I still say Psalm 91 two or three times a day, as my grandmother taught me, and it never fails to comfort me and give me strength. My grandmother insisted Psalm 91 would make a snake stand on its tail! Ours was a simple faith and I knew that God loved me and looked after me. I also knew that he saw everything I did, and was sure my wrongdoing would be seen and punished.

I think we took it for granted that we were born into a Christian community, although there were Muslims in our schools. We looked on Jesus as one of us, one of our own, and were very surprised when the missionaries from abroad came to tell us about him. They suggested that we were not taking enough care of 'our man', not giving him enough respect and honour.

Even today I find signs of colonialist thinking in the Church. At the Church of Scotland General Assembly in 1992 I was very surprised to find that no programme had been planned for the many delegates from other countries, either to show them a little of the beautiful city of Edinburgh, or to permit an exchange of ideas with each other. During the Assembly itself two people were chosen to speak on behalf of the delegates; one a British bishop and the other a priest from India, who claimed that the British had brought Christianity to India, apparently forgetting that the Apostle Thomas had brought the Good News many centuries before that – quite a few centuries before it reached Britain itself! He did not even mention the Indian Mar Thoma Church, one of the earliest churches of all.

When the Israeli occupation of East Jerusalem in June 1967 made communication between the Anglicans in Israel and the Archbishop in Jerusalem easier, we started to talk about reuniting the diocese, i.e. reuniting those of us who remained in Israel with our brothers and sisters in Jordan, Lebanon and Syria. We felt it was time that one of our own should become Bishop in Jerusalem. Dr Root conceded that the subject had been broached in Canterbury. At one point there was a suggestion that it might be a good idea to invite someone from Africa or India to be our bishop as an intermediate step! We did not agree.

'Why should we be good priests and vicars and not make good bishops?' we asked. 'After all, St George, the patron saint of England, came from Palestine!'

After the Six Day War I was also upset at the way Christians in the world reacted to the Israeli victory. We heard stories of church bells ringing in triumph. I felt that there was a lack of Christian feeling for the victims of the war. I preached an emotional sermon on the text 'Not by power, but by my Spirit, saith the Lord'. Some of the expatriate English-speaking members of the congregation, most of them from the hospital run by the Edinburgh Medical Missionary Society, stopped coming to the services. The Archbishop asked an expatriate chaplain from Haifa, the Revd Ronald Adeney, to lead an English service in Christ Church for these people every Sunday evening. One Sunday I sat with Ronald and told him, 'Ronald, this is your last day at Christ Church. After this, you will come only at my invitation.'

'But the Archbishop told me . . .' he said.

'You know the Anglican tradition,' I interrupted, 'I am the vicar here. I can lead a service in English – my English is better than the Arabic of all the missionaries in town. I would be happy to have you as a guest preacher occasionally, when I invite you. Otherwise you don't need to come, OK?'

He reported our conversation to the Archbishop, who came to St Margaret's School and called me for an interview. (St Margaret's was a girls' school run by the diocese in the town.) In the early years of my ministry Archbishop MacInnes used to make St Margaret's his first destination, and called me to come there if he wanted to speak to me. I made it clear to him that I would be extremely happy to see the expatriates in church as members of our community; but there was one congregation in Nazareth, not two.

'And another thing, next time you come to Nazareth', I said, 'I am not coming to St Margaret's to see you. I expect you to come to the church. I am your representative here, I am Vicar of Christ Church and I am entitled at least to the same relationship with you as you have with the missionary ladies of St Margaret's. I hope you will encourage the other ladies to relate to the local church community in town like Hilda Jones does. If they want to live in an English community, they should go back to England.'

St Margaret's was staffed by three ladies from the Church Missionary Society. Two of the British ladies did not come to my services, although one of them, Miss Hilda Jones, took a great interest in the work of the parish and was elected a member of the Pastorate Committee. Neither of the other two came, however. When I saw them I used to ask them why. They made excuses, saying they were busy, they didn't have time to come. I discovered later, quite by chance, that the Archbishop (now Archbishop Appleton) sent his chaplain from Jerusalem to St Margaret's once a month for the sole purpose of giving these two ladies communion. I debated the issue with the Archbishop. 'This is not the Anglican tradition,' I said. 'A priest is appointed to the whole congregation. Since when do some of the congregation decide that they will take communion separately?'

nine *How shall they hear without a preacher?*

'The Spirit of the Lord is upon me, because he has anointed me to preach the good news to the poor. He has sent me to proclaim release to the captives and recovery of sight to the blind, to let the oppressed go free, to proclaim the year of the Lord's favour.'
(LUKE 4.18, 19)

In Nazareth Jesus Christ has always seemed particularly close, and his words to the Nazarenes are daily before me. The verses from the Gospel of Luke quoted above are painted in gold on the wall behind the altar in my church. Jesus was not indifferent to the sufferings of his people. And now they are oppressed and in need of good news. They are prisoners of their fate and blind to a way out of their captivity.

Following his example, I knew that I would have to do what I could to help my people in their struggle for recognition of their rights, for equality, security and dignity. Almost as a matter of course, I became involved in local politics. Many of those young Palestinian Arabs in Israel who had been privileged to study, whether in Israel or abroad, and whatever profession they had chosen, felt obliged to become leaders of their community in some way. We were the first generation which had grown up in Israel; it was up to us to make a place for ourselves in this new country. There were few we could look to for guidance.

The remnant of a people

After the flight or expulsion of nearly three-quarters of a million Palestinians from their homes in 1948 the community was fragmented and lost many of its traditional leaders. In those days there were few cars and fewer telephones, there was no television or local radio, and the number of people who could read was limited. The Palestinians who remained behind were isolated, cut off from each other nearly as much as they were cut off from those outside Israel.

In the villages the style of life was still very simple, governed by the seasons, seed time and harvest. When these people lost their land, their whole way of life changed. In the village, the priest, the *sheikh* and the teacher were accorded honour, as were one's parents and all older people. They were responsible for keeping the peace and settling disputes in the community. On the loss of their land, their sons and daughters were forced to look for work outside the village. Many villages had been totally destroyed in 1948 and the residents forced to move to the towns. Nazareth itself changed almost overnight from a sleepy little town of about ten thousand souls, all of whom were known to each other, to a 'city' which now, fifty years later, has a population of nearly 60,000. Ironically, in the early days of the State many young men from Galilee, who had lost their living on their own land, ended up as seasonal farm labourers in Ramleh and Lydda in the centre of the country, where the Palestinians had been expelled altogether. There was no one left to pick the harvests of olives and citrus fruits in this fertile region of the country.

Those who found no work on the land went into the cities and became unskilled labourers. They mixed with Israelis from many different countries and brought back new customs and ideas which the older people found threatening. There is nothing unusual about this development, which has taken place nearly all over the world. The extraordinary feature of it is that the new ways were identified with the occupier, the enemy. This made it doubly difficult for the young people to cope with the change. They were not only casting off the ways of their parents; they were taking on the ways of the oppressors of their people. It felt very much like betrayal.

During Ottoman times *mukhtars*, or village elders, had been responsible for collecting the taxes from the village and paying them to the government, and for maintaining law and order in the village. The mukhtar was the government representative in the village. He usually came from a large and respected family. The mukhtar was rewarded for his services by means of tax reductions and other, minor privileges. He was the overseer of the village and was able to inform on heads of competing families. This system was kept on by the British, who began to codify the system and introduced local councils which were based on traditional 'councils of elders', in which heads of families in a village came together to discuss village disputes. The mukhtar was kept on as the direct government representative in each village.

The British gradually established other forms of local government. These were municipal councils, local councils and village councils, depending on the size of the towns and villages served. Councillors were elected, but there were restrictions on the right to vote, which was dependent on a minimum tax payment, a minimum age of 25 years and was restricted to men. The councils were still made up of representatives of the wealthy, traditionally powerful families, who fought each other for influence and privileges and made little investment in agricultural reform or in health and other services.

After the 1948 war almost all the Palestinian Arab middle and upper classes had left the country. Those remaining were subject to the military government, which intervened directly in local activities in all the Arab towns and villages: the choice of mukhtars; granting special privileges to certain individuals or groups; planting informers in all villages and following the policy of divide and rule among kin groups and religious sects. Even today our communities are divided along lines of family and religion. A sheikh of the Druze community, for example, still has more influence among Israeli Druze than an Israeli government official.

Those chosen to be mukhtars were not always natural leaders, but were chosen because they were weak enough to be manipulated.

Government officials, including police and security officers, who visited a village expected to be entertained by the mukhtar, and even sent lists of foods they expected to be served – so many chickens, a sheep, a certain number of eggs, etc. – so that the cost of entertaining them often exceeded the salary the mukhtar received for his task. During the meal the mukhtar was expected to report on the villagers, their private lives, subversive activities and the like. No wonder there was often little love lost between the mukhtars and the villagers.

However, over a period of time, Palestinians in Israel became better educated and began to take a more active role in the politics of the country. This activity was often channelled through local councils and local representatives.

The Communist Party

There was one other representative the Palestinians could turn to in those days – the Israeli Communist Party. In order to understand the role the Communist Party plays in Israeli politics we have to go back to the early years of the State, or even earlier. In the 1920s the Palestinian Communist Party provided an alternative to the traditional, conservative leadership in the Arab sector. Under pressure from the Soviet Union, in November 1947 the Communist Party accepted the United Nations partition plan and after the establishment of the State of Israel joined with the Jewish communists to form the Israeli Communist Party. From the beginning of the State, Arab Palestinians were members of Parliament representing the Jewish–Arab Communist Party. Palestinian Arab members of the Communist Party were among the few refugees allowed to return to their homes after 1948. They saw the strength of socialist ideals in Israeli society – the kibbutzim and moshavim, for example, and hoped to participate in the building of a just society for all its members.

The communists were also active at the local government level, and in 1975 had been represented in the Nazareth municipality for the past 37 years, without ever having gained the majority in a council dominated by members of the more traditional Arab community who were members of the ruling Israeli Labour Party. The communists were viewed with suspicion by the majority of the citizens of Nazareth, mainly because they were considered atheists. Those governing Nazareth used the term communist to demonize people who opposed their policies and methods. Even I was labelled a communist, although I was never a member of the Communist Party.

Many Muslims and Christians, although dissatisfied with their current representatives, found it impossible to give their loyalty to a party which proclaimed itself atheist – and anyway it is difficult to live as an atheist in a country which does not know civil marriage! The Communist Party had one great advantage, however: it was not associated with any of the traditional communities. Apart from their past failings, the leaders of the various traditional communities represented only their own local or religious groups, and they had few common interests. The Communist Party promised cohesion and unity. It also appeared to be in opposition to the government.

On 1 May, International Labour Day, the Communist Party organized mass demonstrations under such slogans as 'Down with Military Rule!' Young people like myself were highly impressed by the crowds and the force of such slogans. It was not until quite a lot later that we realized that in demanding an end to military rule we were also assenting to the annexation of Galilee and its integration into the Israeli state.

It also became apparent later that the communists were as little interested in the needs of their supporters as the traditional leaders. Their loyalty to Moscow earned them the nickname of 'His Master's Voice' – a recording made in the Soviet Union and played back in Nazareth. And although the Communist Party did unite people from all the other disunited communities, it split the community along different lines and thus added another segment to an already fragmented society.

The PLO

Outside Israel a body was forming which was to provide us with an example of what could be achieved through unity – the Palestinian Liberation Organization. And in 1968 an event took place which was psychologically very important for the Palestinians. Until then, Israeli forces had regularly crossed the river Jordan and carried out punitive raids on Palestinian refugee camps in Jordan – usually meeting no resistance. In 1968 they attacked the Palestinian camp in Karameh, but this time the Palestinian *fedayeen* put up a strong fight and there were many casualties on both sides.

This was the era of spectacular actions by the PLO designed to draw the world's attention to the plight of the Palestinian people. Suddenly, wherever we went in the world, as soon as it became apparent that we were Palestinians, we were viewed as possible terrorists. Again we were forced to look at ourselves, at our own position.

Growing resistance

I personally have always rejected violence in all its forms. But suddenly many of us found ourselves defending acts and statements, certain forms of behaviour formerly alien to us. After all, my brother was living in Lebanon, subject to Israeli air raids against 'nests of terrorists'. Kamal Nasser, assassinated as a terrorist by the Israelis, was a Palestinian poet and member of the Anglican Church. His assassins used not one but many bullets to kill him, shooting him in the mouth and in his right hand. How long should we remain passive victims?

A new feeling of hope and optimism began to grow among Palestinians outside Israel, and since we were now able to contact our relatives and friends in the West Bank and Gaza, this feeling communicated itself to us inside Israel. The Palestinians in the Occupied Territories were resisting the 'Jordanization' of the West Bank, thinking that King Hussein was encouraged by Israel to do so to secure a 'United Kingdom', i.e. of Jordan and the West Bank.

Local council meetings in the 1950s and 1960s dealt mainly with municipal matters, but in the 1970s, after the abolition of military rule and in the aftermath of the 1967 war, the councils began to realize that these issues could not be dealt with satisfactorily without dealing with the status of the Arab minority as a whole, and even with the problems of Palestinians living outside the country. Thus the local councils became the representatives of the Palestinian minority in national questions.

In Nazareth, September 1970, thousands demonstrated against

the Jordanian Government for the way it handled the uprising of the Palestinians living in Jordan, and later against the Lebanese militias supported by Israel for their massacre of Palestinians in the Sabra and Shatilla refugee camps in 1982. And maybe because we felt even less certain than others of our identity, because as Christians we feared we were less Arab and as Israelis we feared we were less Palestinian, we Christians in Israel became most fervently Arab and most ardently Palestinian.

The Democratic Front

Carried along by the spirit of social and political reawakening among the Palestinian people, young people in Nazareth started to debate how to harness the energy set free by the new climate of optimism. We were doctors, lawyers, pharmacists, architects and teachers. Some of us had studied at the Hebrew University in Jerusalem. Others, like myself, had studied abroad. I had returned from India in 1964, and was ordained priest in 1965. We were all in the process of establishing ourselves in our relevant fields. And we were the new elite, our people looked to us to bring about changes and improvements in their conditions.

We were all about the same age, Muslims and Christians together, although there were more Christians than Muslims. I was nominated to the executive committee of the trade union, where we spoke of the need for change in the local authority. This was the local council which was headed by Saifeddin Zou'abi – and he was not happy with us.

We started by offering our help to the local council. We wanted to put our knowledge at the disposal of the town. We were the intellectuals of the community and we felt that we had much to offer and that much was expected of us. Unfortunately, Saifeddin Zou'abi expelled us from his office.

We continued to meet, discuss and debate, often all through the night. We criticized the local council for not dealing with the problem of sewage – which flowed through the streets in open canals – the problem of refuse disposal or the traffic problem. We took up the issue of the local reservoir, which was uncovered and being polluted. At a meeting with us the District Commissioner of the Ministry of the Interior for Northeast Israel (Galilee),

Israel Koenig, admitted that the municipal council was not carrying out its duties as it should. He revealed that many of the townspeople were not paying local taxes or water rates, that there were about 2,000 rooms in the town which were not registered (council tax was based on the number of rooms in a building) and that 6,700 square metres of building area for commercial use and about 2,000 square metres of trading areas remained untaxed.

We complained that the standard of education in the municipal high school was well below that of other high schools in the town, and that the church was not getting enough support from the local council in the admirable work it was doing in the field of education. Education was a service which was supposed to be provided by the state, but grants to the Arab local councils were often barely enough to cover the cost of rent for the school buildings and the teachers' salaries. There was certainly nothing left over for libraries, laboratories or services such as counsellors.

We sent letters to all the local representatives of the established parties, inviting them to join with us in a broad coalition for the good of the city, but the only party to respond positively was the Communist Party. Finally we came up with a constitution for a Democratic Front made up of the Communist Party, the Graduate Union, the University Students' Association and the Nazareth Trade Union. In August 1974 we called for the resignation of the mayor and declared that the Democratic Front would stand for election.

Suad's uncle, the writer and Member of Knesset for the Communist Party, Emile Habiby, had previously proposed my name for mayor. For a while, I considered running for this office but after a lengthy consultation with Archbishop Appleton decided against it. So my name was put at the bottom of the list of candidates – a position of honour, though symbolic, since it is usual to field double the number of candidates to seats. Thus I was number 34 on the list of the Nazareth Democratic Front.

In December 1975 we won 11 of the 17 seats on the city council. Five of these seats went to members of the Graduate Union and six to the Communist Party. It was our hour of triumph. However, not everybody was happy with our success. In my parish, many of the members had worked for, and with, the old local council, and resented my involvement in its overthrow. Some of my parishioners went as far as to threaten to remove their dead from the Anglican cemetery because of me! Bishop Quba'in received several letters complaining of my 'communist' activities. Luckily he was active himself in the cause of justice for the Palestinians, and respected my goals.

Whenever I was asked how I, as a priest, could cooperate with communists, I always said that Christ did not die only for the capitalists, He died for the communists too, and we have a mission to them. We cannot view them as outside the possibility of salvation.

After our victory in the 1975 municipal elections many journalists, including one from *Time* magazine, who gave his article the title 'Red Star Over Nazareth', wanted to know whether we were going to demand autonomy for the Arab sector in Israel, or even to be part of a Palestinian state. Certainly all kinds of exciting ideas were circulating at the time and we were very aware of our own strength as Palestinians. We realized that representation at local government level was the best opportunity we could have for expressing our national aspirations.

We formed committees to look into the housing problems in the Arab sector and to investigate discrimination against the Arab sector in the allocation of government funds. We also looked for ways to contact Palestinians living outside the country. As part of our quest for our identity we looked for ways to increase awareness of our cultural roots and to commemorate those who had made an outstanding contribution to our cause. This was something new in the Arab sector.

With others, the Graduate Union established a fund in the memory of Dr Anis Kardosh, one of the leaders of the Union, whose untimely death from leukaemia on the eve of our election victory in 1975 was a great blow to the movement. We decided that since Dr Kardosh had always looked on education as a priority in the Arab sector, we would set up a fund for student scholarships to bear his name. We also campaigned for a street in Nazareth to be named after him – a first in the history of the town. The street which leads from Mary's Well to his house is now called Dr Anis Kardosh Street.

When the Palestinian journalist and poet Rashid Hussein died under mysterious circumstances in New York in 1977, I was asked to speak at his funeral. Rashid Hussein was an Israeli Palestinian from the village of Musmus, near Nazareth, who had been living in exile since 1966. Although I had read some of his work, I did not know a lot about him. Now I discovered that he had been a member of the Mapam for many years and had worked in their Nazareth office, writing for their magazine *Al Mirsad*. Disappointed with the party, and despairing of being able to work effectively in Israel, he went to the United States and worked for the Palestinian information agency *Wafa*. It took some effort to convince the Israelis that his body should be allowed home for burial.

It seemed to me that here was someone whose contribution to our cultural heritage should be honoured in some way. Others agreed, so when we went to be with his family on the occasion of his memorial service (it is our tradition to honour the dead with a memorial service forty days after the funeral), we started to discuss ways of keeping his memory alive. It was agreed that we should collect as many of his works as we could find, from at home and from New York where he had been living. Our own publishing house, *Al Sawt*, published two volumes of his collected works.

The Society of Friends of the Prisoners was established to help political prisoners and their families. We asked local people to donate to it. Some of the Christian congregations contributed collections, and some of the money given to charity during the Muslim holy month of Ramadan was earmarked for this purpose. Palestinians abroad contributed through the Welfare Association in Geneva, a large fund for all Palestinians from which we also received support. Then we appealed to other friends abroad. Christian Aid in the Netherlands gave generously, as did the United Holy Land Fund in the United States.

The Society gave practical help to the families where it could. Our own Christ Church School accepted two children from a prisoner's family without asking fees. To mark their religious festivals (they were Muslims) we gave the mother a gift of money for the children. In this way we could help her buy them necessities such as clothes without hurting her feelings. Individuals like myself did what they could for the prisoners by covering the cost of 'coupons'. These coupons were given to the prisoners each month in lieu of pocket money. They used them to buy news-papers, cigarettes, soft drinks, sweets and snacks from a kiosk in the prison.

I once asked a prisoner how they decided who should get the coupons, since there were never enough to go around. He laughed.

'Look,' he said, 'if we get ten coupons and there are a hundred of us in prison, we share the coupons one between ten. Don't worry, every one gets his share!'

This is something I have heard again and again. While in deten-tion the prisoners practise solidarity and behave in a very disci-plined manner. Many use the time to educate themselves and those who have knowledge to share pass it on to others. I wish this exemplary behaviour was copied by those outside. Too often our best efforts are thwarted by petty jealousy and rivalry. The Friends of the Prisoners is a case in point.

All went well until we had enough money to help in a substantial way. In order to get maximum benefit from the money, we decided to give it in the form of a loan to ex-prisoners who wanted to set up in business. Since it is difficult for Arabs to find a decent job in Israel at the best of times, and ex-prisoners are not sought-after employees, this was an appropriate solution in many cases. Inevitably, not all these businesses were an immediate success. Some did not succeed at all. There was an argument among members of the Society, some of whom wanted to forgive the prisoners their debts, at least for a while. Others insisted that the loan system would not work if we did not enforce repayment. The logical conclusion of this latter argument was that we should take ex-prisoners to court if they did not or could not repay their loan. In Israel, insolvent debtors are sent to prison. To some of us, this did not seem the ideal rehabilitation programme.

Some members of the Democratic Front, including myself, felt that Galilee needed a university, and that it should be built in Nazareth. We wanted it to be an Arab university, specializing in Arabic language and literature, and holding courses in Arabic.

Since Arabic is an official language of Israel and Arabic speakers make up 17 per cent of the population,[1] this seemed only reasonable to us. We collected money and drew up a curriculum which received much acclaim in academic circles. I still have copies of the curriculum in my office at Christ Church, and I am still hoping that we might one day receive government permission to build our university. Until now the only answer from the government was that Arab students from Galilee could study at the Haifa University or the other Israeli universities. Government representatives with whom we spoke admitted freely that they were convinced that an Arab university in Galilee would become a breeding ground for nationalism and dissatisfaction. Luckily my father taught me patience, and I still hope that my son may be able to participate in the completion of the project I helped to initiate.

Meanwhile Palestinians in the West Bank and Gaza caught the flavour of our enthusiasm and came to congratulate us in their hundreds. In fact during the first couple of months after the election we were much too busy receiving delegations to get on with the work we were elected to do. But those were heady days and nobody was in a mood to criticize. After the years of frustration we were swept away on a wave of euphoria.

In 1976 Israel allowed municipal elections to take place in the West Bank and Gaza. To her surprise, the population of the Occupied Territories expressed overwhelming support for the Palestinian Liberation Organization. Now it was our turn to visit them and congratulate them on their courage and unity. For the first time since 1948 Palestinians inside and outside Israel were united and working together for a better future for all of us.

We started to organize work camps in Galilee. Young people from the West Bank joined us in our efforts to develop our district. Students came from Bir Zeit and the other West Bank universities. They stayed in our homes. In the evenings we sang together, held poetry readings, and, of course, there were many speeches. Finally we were really getting to know each other again, after nearly 30 years of separation.

Within Israel a crisis point was reached in 1976, when the Israeli government declared its intention to expropriate 20,000 *dunums* of Arab land, part of it a fertile plain belonging to the Arab villages of Arrabeh, Sakhnin and Deir Hanna, in Galilee. On 30 March 1976, the Committee for the Defence of Arab Land, of which I was an active member, led a demonstration protesting against the massive confiscation of Arab land. We persuaded the leaders of the Arab sector to support a general strike on the same day. In Nazareth only one or two shops opened in defiance of the strike. Bus drivers were persuaded to refuse to take the workers to their places of employment in Tel Aviv and Haifa, and the schools were closed. Almost the whole town was out in the streets. The security forces were also there, with armoured vehicles and even tanks. There was an anger in the eyes of the soldiers which boded ill.

We started receiving reports of clashes between demonstrators and security forces in the Triangle and in some of the Galilee villages, especially Deir Hanna, Sakhnin and Arrabeh. We heard rumours of several deaths and hundreds wounded. I became very worried, so I rushed through the streets towards Mary's Well and the home of the mayor, hoping for more reliable information. I saw a tank heading for the same house, followed by thousands of young people, including children. It was obviously an explosive situation, where the young people could only get hurt, so I called on them to go home. It seemed very possible that the armed forces were only waiting for an excuse to open fire, and a stone thrown by a youth could provide that very excuse.

The mayor's wife came out and tried to defend her home – the soldiers were pulling up plants and hurling plant pots to the ground – and there was a fight. Some of the older people present and I did our best to calm the situation. Then I heard that injured people were being turned away from the hospitals, so a friend drove me to the Nazareth Hospital. The authorities had decreed that no one who could not pay the costs immediately should be treated. So I left a blank cheque at this hospital and went to the other two hospitals in town, where I did the same, to ensure at least that the wounded were treated.

By the end of the day, six of our people had been shot dead: one from the Triangle area, one from Cana of Galilee and four from

Deir Hanna, Sakhnin and Arrabeh, which became known as the Land Day Triangle. There were roadblocks and a curfew had been declared.

The episode revealed once again the stubbornness of the Israeli officials and the brutality of the armed forces – the Israeli Defence Force which was supposed to defend us, the citizens of Israel. it also became a landmark in the process of the Arab minority towards a willingness to stand up for their rights.

On 24 May the National Committee of Chairmen of Local Arab Authorities sent the following memorandum to the Prime Minister of Israel:

> The Arabs are citizens of the state and believe that there is no substitute for living together in peace and full understanding between Jews and Arabs in the country of Israel and in all the countries of the Middle East... The incidents of 30 March (Land Day) were, to a great extent, an expression of the problems that have accumulated among the Arabs of Israel. The Arabs of Israel remained on their lands trusting the sincerity of the promise of full equality made in the Declaration of Independence. We turn to the government through you, Mr Prime Minister, with the following request...
>
> A. Suspension of all confiscations announced for Galilee and the Triangle.
> B. Transfer of all state lands within the jurisdiction of local authorities to the ownership of local authorities.
> C. Transfer of all Muslim *waqf* properties to a Muslim committee appointed by Arab local authorities.
> D. Closing down of all Arab Departments, which are, in the eyes of Arab citizens, a symbol of discrimination and an obstacle to the integration of Arabs into the country. The establishment of an Advisory Committee on Arab Education in the Office of the Minister of Education to be composed of elected members rather than appointed officials.
> E. The establishment of a Co-ordinating Committee in the Office of the Prime Minister which will include representatives from selected Arab local authorities, for the purpose of dealing with the neglected issues of the Arab population of Israel.

F. Closing the police files on individuals who took part in the events of Land Day.

G. Establishing a national investigating commission to look into the events of Land Day.[2]

In his reply, Prime Minister Rabin stressed the fact that Israel was a Jewish state and that it was obliged to grant the Arabs full rights as a unique cultural and religious entity, but he refused to make any commitments concerning land, not even with regard to confiscations planned for the future. The Committee was not satisfied with this reply, especially the emphasis on the Jewish character of the state and the description of the Arabs in Israel as a cultural and religious minority (rather than a national minority). They replied:

Your Excellency's clear response that Israel is a Jewish state whose purpose and aims are the realization of Zionist yearnings while safeguarding the equal rights of the Arabs in the areas of culture and religion leads us to fear that this declaration regarding our status as an Arab nation in Israel, this incomplete perception, will lead to treating the Arabs as subjects and not as citizens with equal rights. We feel, and we ask Your Excellency to respect this feeling, that we are equal partners in the country, and that the Israeli–Arab conflict can in no way justify any lessening of the right of the Arabs to equality and the recognition of their national affiliation, which is an historical fact ... We have great confidence in the victory of democracy and justice, and we believe that co-existence in peace and brotherhood in Israel between the two nations is an historical imperative and should be realized in such a way as to serve the interests of peace. We should decrease existing points of conflict and find solutions to them. The major point of contention which is liable to lead to the danger of the two nations drawing further apart is the denial of our status as a national minority and the failure to recognize our right to keep the land on which our forefathers lived, as well as the lack of concern for promoting the level of local services on the basis of equality, and the absence of co-ordination with the Arab local authorities regarding the subject of planning and development in our villages in the areas of agriculture, industry and housing.

The 30th of March, now known as Land Day, has since been commemorated each year as a symbol of our suffering and willingness to suffer for our land. It was a success in that the decision to expropriate the land was suspended. To this day the Arab farmers continue to work their land, but I admit I am disappointed in the form the remembrance takes. Instead of going out to the land, to work on it and celebrate it, Land Day has become a day for long speeches of self-congratulation on the part of our political representatives, while those who were injured receive no support. Some of those who were active in the demonstration were taken to court for obstructing the armed forces and faced stiff fines and court costs which they could not pay alone. In one case, a man had his leg amputated as a result of injuries sustained during the strike. Another victim, the father of 12 children, was brought to my attention on Eid Al Fitr, the big Muslim feast day. He was in such financial straits that he was unable to buy food for the feast.

Later we started the Land Fund to commemorate Land Day in a more meaningful way. The most important thing was to cultivate the land, to strengthen our claim to it, so we started to collect money for olive seedlings. In the first year we planted 3,000 olive seedlings, and the number has since grown to over 10,000. Many joined hands to help the Land Fund appeal, some giving one seedling, others hundreds, but we still need more – not only olives, but fig trees, almond trees and agricultural equipment to make the land arable.

In the matter of the Land Fund I personally was influenced a great deal by what I learned from the Jews. At first, when we tried to get support from the local community we were viewed as day-dreamers. But I looked at how the Jewish community unites to support Israel and I did not despair that our brothers and sisters in the Church would come to our aid. Jewish families or groups donate a forest, I thought, or some trees for a kibbutz, and their names are to be found all over the country on commemorative plaques. Why shouldn't our people come together to do something similar for an Arab village? So we put the idea to the test. We sent a circular to friends all over the world, and the response enabled us to buy those first 3,000 seedlings.

In the meantime, the Judaization of Galilee continues apace, with more and more hilltops sporting so-called 'observation settlements'. I have never heard officially what they are supposed to observe, but since the only thing to see apart from the birds are the Arab villages on the slopes below them, I presume it is the latter. As the new Jewish towns grow they swallow the land of Arab villagers – but without swallowing the villagers themselves, as the example of Ramya shows.

Ramya is one of forty or so unrecognized villages in Israel. Its inhabitants live on land which they claim is theirs by right although they cannot prove it. Since the village is not recognized it is not connected to the electricity and water supplies, or to a sewage system.

Now, the nearby new town of Karmiel wants to expand and cover the land of Ramya. Ramya's residents have expressed their willingness to become part of Karmiel, but the town wants the land without its inhabitants. Due to public pressure the Israeli government recently offered the inhabitants of Ramya a small plot of land per family to build a house on, but the land will not be in Karmiel, which is for Jews only. Arabs are only allowed to work there, not to live there.

In the history of Israel I cannot point to one town or settlement Israel has built for its Arab citizens, whereas hundreds have been built for the Jewish community. As long as land management in Israel is in the hands of the Jewish National Fund, which aims to reclaim as much of the land of Eretz Israel as possible for the Jewish people and forbids the sale of land to Arab Israelis, it will be extremely difficult for us to redress this imbalance.

I have always loved children and young people, and my first training was as a teacher, so it was inevitable that I should get involved in children's issues. In my own neighbourhood I had discussions with neighbours who did not wish the local children to play in the alleys in front of our houses, although there is no park or playground for them to play in, and therefore no alternative. In the Occupied Territories the children were much worse off, having no play areas or toys at all. I started to take a special interest in the conditions in which these children were growing up. This interest soon brought to my ears stories of mistreatment of children by the armed forces.

I had been forbidden to enter the West Bank and Gaza Strip since 1984, but some American citizens who were working closely with me – one of whom was a psychiatrist of Arab background – began to visit the occupied territories and talk to children who had been detained by the armed forces there. They recorded their findings in the form of interviews (with the names of the children changed for their protection) and published these in a brochure to which I wrote an introduction. We publicized it through church contacts, and sent it to the different embassies, Jewish peace organizations, Amnesty International, and the United States Human Rights Commission. The report became so well known that it was referred to at the United Nations during the hearing on World Children's Day in 1988, the Year of the Child.

I heard of no direct reaction by the Israeli authorities until a representative of a European embassy came to me with a copy of a letter signed by Ms Tamar Gaulan, Director of the Human Rights Department of the Ministry of Justice. Instead of responding to the accusations in the brochure she tried to persuade the embassy that I was a PLO stooge and therefore not to be trusted.

I could not let this go without comment, so we organized a press conference at the American Colony Hotel in Jerusalem. It was crowded with journalists and cameramen. I referred to the Gospel of Mark 10.13–16, in which Jesus says: 'Let the little children come to me; do not stop them; for it is to such as these that the kingdom of God belongs.' We brought three very brave children to speak for themselves about their experiences, and everyone was most impressed by their courage and honesty as they told how they had been handled by the authorities in prison. Shortly afterward the Landau Commission conducted its investigations and produced its famous report criticizing the treatment of Palestinian detainees in Israeli prisons.

* * *

During this period of closeness with Palestinians from the West Bank and Gaza we became more aware that we were one people, and Palestinians in Israel started to cast off the label of Israeli Arab, and call themselves Palestinians; sometimes we used terms like Israeli Palestinians, but we insisted that we were not just part of the Arab nation, we belonged specifically to the Palestinian people.

In Nazareth, this brought us into conflict with the Communist Party, which was for the international solidarity of the workers and against national goals. The Communists had always identified themselves as Israeli Arabs. There were other tensions within the Democratic Front. Membership of the Graduate Union ws open to any man or woman who was a graduate born or residing in Nazareth, or having worked in Nazareth for not less than two years. Many communists fulfilled these requirements and became members of the Graduate Union. Some of the members of the Graduate Union were already members of the Communist Party, for which there is an historical explanation. The Greek Orthodox Church had always had close ties with the Russian Orthodox Church, which ran several educational seminaries in the Holy Land, including the one in Nazareth (the Moscobiyeh) which I have already mentioned. Some of the students of these seminaries were sent in the early years of the twentieth century to complete their studies in Russia, and some of them came back in the 1920s influenced by political developments there. It was they who, together with Jewish immigrants from the USSR, established the Communist Party of Palestine. Thus there was a tradition of sympathy for the communist movement among the well-educated in the Greek Orthodox community.

The same was true of the other member organizations of the Democratic Front – the Students' Association and the Trades Union. Both were open to the communists. Thus when there was a difference of opinion within the Front on an issue, some of our members had divided loyalties, and the Communist Party exerted pressure on them to toe the party line, which many did. Since the Communist Party was receiving substantial financial backing from the Soviet Union, it was able to offer incentives to its members, such as scholarships or opportunities for study in the Eastern European countries for members of their families.

More and more communists became members of the Graduate Union, until those of us who were not communists were outnumbered, and many started to withdraw from the organization, feeling that it no longer represented their views. In 1980 we reluctantly decided that we had no other choice but to call for a split, and 76 of us formally resigned from the organization.

For me, the differences came to a head when leaders of the Democratic Front for Peace and Equality asked me to sign a statement of policy calling for a Palestinian state to be established beside the Israeli state within the boundaries of 4 June 1967, a position I could not and cannot accept. The boundaries of Israel and Palestine must be negotiated by the representatives of the two nations, it is not for us to prejudge the issue.

It was a difficult decision to make, and many criticized us for dividing the Arab minority, but we felt it was a move we had to make. I think history has proved us right. The communist ideals have not proved successful in practice anywhere in the world, but of course in 1981, when we decided to make the break, we did not dream that the communist system would collapse even in the Soviet Union.

ten *Coal for the cause*

*A group of Palestinians was discussing their future. 'Imagine', said
one of them, 'our cause is a train. What job would you like to have
on it?' 'I would like to be the driver,' said one man, confidently. 'I
would like to be the signalman and get things started,' said another.
'I would be the guard and make sure everyone was comfortable and
safe on the train,' said another. Another: 'I would work in the
restaurant car and provide food for the journey.'*

One man sat quietly in the corner, saying nothing.

*'Haven't you got anything to offer the cause?' asked the first
man. 'What would you like to be?'*

'I shall be the coal,' he replied.

The Progressive Movement

We did not withdraw from politics but reorganized in order to
address ourselves to the problems facing the community. There
were maybe eleven or twelve of us, including my friend the
lawyer Kamel Daher; Dr Rashid Salim who was once Secretary
General of the Nazareth Democratic Front; the late Fouzi Abdallah, a poet famous within the Arab community and for a time
General Secretary of the Democratic Front; Professor George
Kanaza, the only Arab professor at an Israeli university; and
others.

We sent a note to our colleagues explaining that we were not
satisfied with the organization of the Nazareth Democratic Front

and that we had pledged ourselves to the welfare of Nazareth, not of the Communist Party. Our first circular went out in November 1981, and less than two weeks later Professor Kanaza published an article analysing the malady of the Democratic Front and proposing a remedy. The next day there was an aggressive rebuttal in the communist daily, *Al Ittihad*, which included a personal attack on Professor Kanaza, accusing him of betrayal. That same day we appealed to the people of Nazareth in a circular defending the right of free speech. The circular appeared under the heading *Al Kutla Al Wataniya* – The National Faction. In it we criticized the discriminatory policies of the Israeli government but pointed out that we should also put our own house in order.

It was not an easy decision to take our leave of the Democratic Front which we had helped build up with such enthusiasm and such high hopes. Our new group also faced severe practical difficulties. We had no newspaper, not even a weekly journal with which to reach the public.

Between 11 and 15 November we organized a meeting which was held at the YMCA. I was asked to chair the meeting, and I said that it is not enough to criticize, even though my Protestant background had taught me that protest was good. What we needed was a new road, which would take us to the same goal we had set ourselves and our people in 1974. I spoke of the difficulty of hewing a new road.

That very same evening we decided to change our name from Al Kutla Al Wataniya to Al Haraka Al Taqaddumiya – the Progressive Movement. Our name was intended to demonstrate our openness to change, our will to move forward. Although we stressed that we would focus on the needs of Nazareth, we did stretch out a hand to other villages and communities, appealing to them to join us in our struggle to improve the lot of our people and to increase awareness of our Palestinian identity.

We emphasized that the Palestinian citizens of Israel are also an integral part of the wider Palestinian nation. We aimed at deepening Palestinian consciousness among our people, claiming national minority status in Israel and equal rights with our Jewish fellow citizens. We also demanded recognition of our cultural and historical heritage.

The Movement was fiercely opposed by the Democratic Front, which even went as far as to suggest we were the party that District Commissioner Israel Koenig had spoken of in his memorandum. After our success in the 1976 elections, Koenig wrote a memorandum to the government containing proposals for suppressing the Arabs in Israel. It included suggestions such as encouraging Arabs to study abroad and then making it difficult for them to return to the country. He also proposed a new party to be formed under the auspices of the Zionist Labour bloc which would ostensibly campaign for peace in the region and thus weaken the genuine peace groups in the Israeli Arab population. The memorandum was leaked to the press and caused a scandal because of its racist tone.

We started by publishing a newspaper, which we gave the title 'Solidarity', relating to the events in Poland at that time. Since we did not have a lot of money the newspaper did not appear weekly, but usually once a month and sometimes even once every two months.

In November 1983 we ran for election to the city council. Again I closed the list. In the weeks before the elections our meetings were crowded, with standing room only at the Cinema House (the Cinema House used to be the Cinema Diana, but is now the biggest meeting house in Nazareth), and so many came to our closing meeting that the crowd overflowed and filled the surrounding streets. However, the Progressive Movement had neither the experience nor the resources to defeat the established parties, and we had to be satisfied with four seats in the council – which still represented about 25 per cent of the votes. The Democratic Front won 11 seats.

This was the position when we decided to broaden the Progressive Movement and run for the Knesset. Our platform was based on two main points:

- We believe in the establishment of a Palestinian State to exist beside the State of Israel, the boundaries of the two states to be negotiated by the two parties involved.

- We stand for the right of Palestinian refugees to return to their homes or to receive adequate compensation for their losses.

Both these positions are anchored in United Nations resolutions 242 and 338.

Events in the region were again drawing us closer to Palestinians outside Israel. After the Black September massacre of Palestinians in Jordan in 1970 many *fedayeen* fled to Lebanon, where they joined their brothers and sisters in the refugee camps. Together they started to build an autonomous infrastructure providing the communities with health care, education and protection. Southern Lebanon became known as *Fatahland* after the largest faction of the PLO, Arafat's Fatah. This '*state within the state*', as it came to be known, was a political force which could no longer be dismissed as a 'refugee problem', to be solved by the assimilation of the Palestinians into the populations of the surrounding countries. The Israeli government decided it must be destroyed. This was the real reason for the invasions of Lebanon in 1978 and 1982, known in Israel as Operation Peace for Galilee. Israel did not succeed in destroying the morale of the Palestinians. It did, however, damage the morale of its own soldiers, who were forced to see themselves as the aggressors for the first time in the history of their country. The turning-point came in September 1982, when Lebanese Christian *Phalangists* entered the refugee camps of Sabra and Shatilla to the south of Beirut with the permission – or perhaps on the orders – of the Israeli armed forces. There they brutally murdered some 2,000 women, children and old people left defenceless by the withdrawal of the PLO fighting forces on 30 August of that year.

After the massacre the Progressive Movement immediately organized a meeting to express our solidarity and sympathy with our brothers and sisters in the camps and to draw attention to their sufferings. Israeli society was shocked and various groups came together under the banner of the *Peace Now* movement to protest against the government's policy. There were massive demonstrations in which 400,000 Israeli citizens took to the streets to express their horror at the massacres. They were led by Ashkenazi Jews brought up in the shadow of the Holocaust and distraught to think of Jews involved in such an outrage.

The Progressive List for Peace

We started to discuss our possible role as a bridge between the Jewish and Palestinian communities and decided to make it known that we wished to join hands with progressive Jews with aims and ideals similar to our own. We made it clear from the very beginning that ours would be an Arab–Jewish and not a Jewish–Arab coalition, since it was clear that we would always find more support among the Arab community than among the Jews. We received a response from *Alternativa*. This was a group headed by Matti Peled (Dr Mattityahu Peled, a lecturer at Tel Aviv University), Uri Avneri and Yaakov Arnon. During the siege of the city by the Israeli forces, Uri Avneri, who is a journalist, had met and interviewed the leader of the PLO, Chairman Arafat, in Beirut, and in July 1982 we had invited him to address the public in the Cinema House and tell us about the meeting.

In various forms, particularly as the Israeli Council for Israeli–Palestinian Peace, this group had been working for peace between Israel and the Palestinian people for years. They accepted that this could only come about if the Palestinians could determine their own future, and thus supported the Palestinian wish for a state of their own. They also recognized the PLO as the sole legitimate representative of the Palestinian people.

Together we decided to form the Progressive List for Peace (PLP), which would be composed of two factions, the Progressive Movement and Alternativa. The Progressive Movement asked Muhammad Miari to be our first candidate. Muhammad had been an active nationalist for many years, first with the Al Ard group and later with the Committee for the Defence of Arab Land. We had been members of the Follow-Up Committee for the Galilee University together and Miari was a founding member of Al Sawt. He had made a name for himself when he was arrested in 1983 on his return from an NGO meeting on the Question of Palestine, organized by the United Nations in Geneva, accused of meeting with Yassir Arafat.

With our Jewish partners we decided that Miari should head the list; Matti Peled would be second; I would be third (I was also elected General Secretary of the party); and Walid Sadek fourth. Haim Hanegbi, a Jew, was to hold fifth place and then places were allotted alternately to Arabs and Jews up to number 120. Uri Avneri closed the list. Of course we knew we would be extremely lucky to win one seat!

In the event it was only after a fight that we were allowed to take part in the elections at all, since the Ministry of the Interior rejected our candidacy. The Israeli Central Elections Committee decided to disqualify us on the grounds that our principles endangered the integrity and existence of the State of Israel, and preservation of its distinctness as a Jewish state. The court of appeal upheld our right to run for election.

Shortly afterwards, as a result of this decision, the Basic Law, which functions as the constitution in Israel, was amended to include the following paragraph:

> A list of candidates shall not participate in the elections for the Knesset if its aims or actions, expressly or by implication, point to one of the following: (1) denial of the existence of the State of Israel *as the state of the Jewish people* . . . [my emphasis]

Therefore, again, it was demonstrated clearly to me that Israel is not the state of its Arab citizens. At the deepest level we are denied the right to feel we belong here.

We won our case on Lailat Al-Qadr, the night on which Muslims celebrate the coming down of the Qur'an to the Prophet Muhammad. We had less than 24 days in which to conduct our election campaign. It was my responsibility to campaign in the Triangle area, and although this is a purely Muslim region, I was overwhelmed at the support I received. We used the forbidden colours of the Palestinian flag, red, white, green and black, and our symbol, the letter 'F' for *Filasteen*, was everywhere. It was like a happy little revolution. I remember going into the Triangle village of Baqa Al-Gharbiyya, where the Arabic 'F' in the four colours lined the streets. It was 11 o'clock at night when I arrived (this was my fourth meeting of the day) but the crowds were still awake and waiting.

'Dear Palestinian sisters!' I cried. There was a round of applause. 'Dear Palestinian brothers,' I continued, 'you remind me of a place to the south of Beirut. Will the young people tell me what that place was called?' '*Fatahland*,' came the reply.

'If the Shin Beth hears you and questions you,' I said, 'tell them you are quoting from the Qur'an the *sura*: "*inna fatahna laka fathan mubiinan*".'

This *sura* speaks of a new opening, a new possibility which is sure to end in success. On the eve of the election, we reminded people that this was the anniversary of the revolution of the Egyptian people led by Gamal Abdel Nasser, a good omen for a new victory of the Arab people.

On 24 July 1984 we won two seats in the Knesset.

Relations with the PLO

In November 1984 the Palestine National Council, the Palestinian Parliament in exile, met in Amman, in Jordan. Palestinians from all over the world attended it, including representatives from the West Bank. This meeting signified a triumph for the PLO, which had been going through a very difficult period after the evacuation from Lebanon and the split with the rejectionist front led by Abu Musa in Syria. The Progressive Movement congratulated the PLO and wished it success in realizing its aims. This message was printed in our own newspaper, *Al Taddamun*, and in the Jerusalem daily *Al Fajr*. The PLP became open in its support for the aspirations of the PLO, and one of our campaigns was to persuade Israel to recognize the PLO as the legitimate representative of the Palestinian people and its negotiating partner on the path to peace.

At the time, the world in general still viewed the PLO as a terrorist organization, so why were we convinced that Israel should negotiate with it? To understand this, we have to understand what the PLO meant to the Palestinian people.

During the Seventies I had travelled widely in Europe. One of the questions most often addressed to me there was how did I, an Israeli citizen of Palestinian background, relate to the PLO. I replied that the Israelis have a representative body – the government of Israel. The Palestinians also have a representative body – the Palestinian Liberation Organization. I cannot claim to speak on behalf of the Israelis, neither can I speak on behalf of the

PLO. I stand in between, and my hope is to become a bridge of understanding between the two communities so that each might recognize the reality that is the other.

In 1972 I was in Berlin as a guest of the *Evangelische Kirche*, the Protestant church in Germany. My host took me to a panel discussion of the Arab–Israeli conflict where the speakers included the Israeli Consul-General, a Palestinian and a Syrian. At the end of the meeting there was to be a collection of money for Israel. The Consul-General described the situation in Israel and gained much sympathy. Then it was the turn of the Palestinian and the Syrian to speak. They spoke very emotionally, accusing the Israelis of fascism and genocide. I could feel that they were doing their cause more harm than good. The audience had stopped listening.

I asked my host if he could arrange for me to speak, which he did. I was introduced as a Palestinian citizen of Israel and a Christian priest. I raised my right hand in a fist and said, 'I am for Israel!' There was some applause. Then I raised my arm again and said, 'I am for Palestine!' Again there was applause, and now the people were alert. I went on to say what I always say – that there can be no peace for Israel without justice for the Palestinian people, that the peace and security of the one nation lies in the peace and security of the other. It was decided to split the money collected and give half to Israel and half to the Palestinians.

The same travels allowed me to meet members of the PLO for the first time and form my own opinion of the organization. From the beginning I made it clear that although I, like all Palestinians, recognize the PLO as the sole legitimate representative of our people, as an Israeli citizen I had absolutely no intention of aligning myself with the organization. I am convinced that the Palestinians who stayed in Israel won the battle lost by those who left their country. Why should I jeopardize my status here?

Mainstream Israelis are constantly willing to see the Arab citizens of the state as a fifth column working for its destruction. I do not wish to feed this suspicion. In the same way as I refused to work for the Israeli security services, I refuse to become involved in any illegal or underhand activities directed against the state. I will fight for the right of the Palestinians in Israel for equality before the law and in society, and I uphold the right of my Palestinian brothers outside Israel to a country of their own. But the road to peace lies in the recognition of realities, including the reality that is Israel, and I will do nothing to harm the cause of peace.

Unknown to me I was later to find out that my attitude was gaining me respect in the PLO.

eleven *Meeting Arafat*

In June 1982, the year of 'Operation Peace for Galilee', the Israeli Defence Forces invaded Lebanon in an attempt to annihilate the PLO, which had its headquarters in Beirut. The city was under siege for two months, but the Israelis could not break the Palestinian resistance. Eventually, the PLO leader negotiated with the Israelis through the mediation of the USA and it was agreed that the Israelis would end the siege if the PLO troops withdrew to the north of Lebanon. In negotiating the withdrawal of Yassir Arafat and his troops, the PLO had received promises from the USA that Israel would not take revenge on the Palestinian civilians left in the refugee camps of the Lebanon. The Israeli armed forces remained in control of West Beirut.

In the autumn of the same year I visited Australia as a guest of the Commission for Peace and Justice of the Uniting Church of Australia, arriving on Friday 17 September, the day when news reached the world of the massacre in the Palestinian refugee camps of Sabra and Shatilla. Lebanese Christian Phalangists entered the camps under the eyes of the Israeli army and murdered two thousand defenceless civilians.

The Commission had organized a press conference for 20 September, at which I was to speak, and in all my life I had never seen such a crowded press conference. Of course I was asked for my views on the events in Beirut, and I stated clearly that Israel must bear responsibility, directly or indirectly, for what had happened. The massacre could not have taken place without their knowledge and approval.

This was later confirmed by eyewitness reports and an Israeli commission of inquiry, whose report became known as the

Kahan Report. Next morning I was asked for an interview by *Good Morning Australia*, an Australian radio programme. Also interviewed was Ali Kazak, the official representative of the PLO in Australia. Ali later asked the Commission if they would agree to my speaking to the Arab community in Australia. With my consent they agreed. Now that I was known, because of the press conference, I was speaking at five, six, seven meetings a day. At one meeting of the Diocesan Synod of Melbourne people spontaneously collected $20,000 towards the cost of sending a medical team to treat the injured and suffering victims of the massacre.

The Arab community arranged a reception for me which was attended by maybe a hundred people. Sometimes Ali would join our church meetings. I asked him to keep me informed on the situation in Beirut, which he did, bringing me copies of the daily telexes which arrived in his office from Lebanon. He also passed on messages of greeting and thanks from leaders of the PLO who appreciated my speaking out. I did not hesitate to call on the government of Australia to recognize the PLO. Again I said we must recognize realities, and the PLO is a reality.

Not everyone appreciated my involvement. Later I learned that the church authorities had organized round-the-clock protection for me after receiving threats from Phalangist and Zionist groups in Australia.

In 1984 I was invited to Geneva to a conference of non-governmental organizations on the question of Palestine, where I spoke on the role of religion in the peace-making process. There I met Maxim Ghillan, a French Jew who publishes a magazine called *Israel & Palestine*. One day he told me that some people would like to meet with me – 'some representatives of the Palestinian people'. 'You mean from the PLO,' I said. Maxim said they wanted to thank me for what I was doing. I told him I had no objection to meeting anyone as long as it was in the open, but I didn't need thanks. Whatever I did, I did it because I believed it was right, not to please anyone else.

That same evening I was invited to a cocktail reception given by Zouhdi Tarazi, the PLO representative to the United Nations. He confirmed that the PLO was interested in what I had to say on the role of the Church in the peace process and my views on a political solution. 'The end of your presentation, where you say that the peace and security of the one depends on the peace and security of the other, was very much appreciated,' he said.

That night I received a telephone call. It was after one o'clock and I had already been asleep, so it took me a while to realize who was talking to me. A man introduced himself as Ghazi Khoury, Abu Faisal. He asked how I was, how the church work was going, and mentioned that he had relatives in Nazareth who were members of my church. He was in Holland, and would like to meet me. I was not able to go to Holland just then because parish duties called in Nazareth.

'Never mind. Feel free to call me any time you are visiting your friends or relatives in Holland,' he said.

Thus began a relationship which eventually led to a visit to Tunis, to meet the chairman of the PLO, Yassir Arafat himself. But in the following months Maxim Ghillan contacted me a few times and Kamel Daher and I went to Paris, where Maxim took us for a magnificent Chinese meal and introduced us to others from the Jewish left. Gradually it was decided that a delegation from the Progressive List for Peace, three Jews and three Arabs, should go to Tunis to meet with Arafat. The six of us were Muhammad Miari and Matti Peled, Yaakov Arnon, Uri Avneri, Kamel Daher and myself.

Our plans evidently did not escape notice. Once when I was in Jerusalem the Bishop came to me and asked what was going on. 'I understand they have a "tap" on your telephone and you may be being followed,' he said. I should mention that the law forbidding Israelis to have contacts with the PLO did not come into force until 1986, after my second visit to Arafat. I did not break this law, although I thought it very foolish and am glad that it was recently repealed. As I told the Bishop, I was doing nothing wrong, or even unusual – Israelis were meeting members of the PLO all over the world. Indeed, how can we solve our differences without dialogue?

This time when we arrived in Paris we were welcomed at Charles de Gaulle airport by three people, two of whom had been present the last time Kamel and I were there. These two were Egyptian Jews who had been in the Egyptian communist party but left

Egypt and settled in France after the 1948 war in Palestine. They were committed to furthering the cause of peace between Jews and Arabs.

The first obstacle to our visit to Tunis was our Israeli passports. These were not recognized by the Tunisian government. Eventually someone came and took our documents from us. We learned that he was a Tunisian. We were offered a drink while we waited, and after a while he returned. 'If you are asked,' he said, 'your names are . . .', and he gave each of us a name. We received tickets in our new names and flew with Air France to Tunis. On arrival we did not show any passports. We were given VIP treatment and driven in a convoy of private cars to a hotel in Sidi Bou Said, a beautiful suburb of Tunis, on the site of ancient Carthage. There I finally met Ghazi Khoury face to face. We did not meet Abu Amar (as Arafat is affectionately known among Palestinians) that first evening, but we met others and the next day were taken to meet Chairman Arafat; the late Abu Iyad, the PLO's foreign minister; Abu Maazen and others. The 'Old Man', Arafat, welcomed us with hugs.

Twelve people took part in the official meeting, our delegation from Israel and Abu Iyad, Abu Mazen, Hakam Balawi, Imad Shakour and Ghazi Khoury, as well as Abu Amar himself. In fact most of those who were responsible for relating to the Israeli peace camp were present.

We spoke of the political platform of the PLP, advocating a two-state solution based on recognition of the State of Israel by the Palestinians and the right of the Palestinian people to a state of their own on Palestinian soil, side by side with Israel. The boundaries of these states would be the subject of negotiations. When my turn came to speak, I opened with a question from my 11-year-old daughter Rania. 'My daughter sends you greetings,' I said. 'She would like to know why you don't come to see us.' Abu Amar laughed heartily and noted her name in his diary.

I went on to ask that the PLO recognize Israel as a reality and that we relate to our differences in a way that makes it easy for the international community and ordinary people to understand that Palestinians are normal human beings, with the same ordinary fears, hopes, aspirations and rights.

Matti Peled asked if Arafat could give us some information about Israeli soldiers missing in action in Lebanon. Arafat promised to do what he could, but unfortunately did not send us the information. Perhaps others did not agree with him that it was a good idea.

After a long meeting – we talked for perhaps three hours – we adjourned for lunch. I noticed that Arafat eats very simply, avoiding sugar and salt, which he regards as poisons. He does not smoke or drink alcohol either. But the food he offered us was excellent and he was a kind and considerate host. Arafat surprised me at one point by asking after my father, who had been in hospital. 'Is he back home yet?' he asked. I had mentioned to one of our contacts that I might not be able to participate in the meeting, because of my father, but I was greatly surprised to find that Arafat knew and remembered about him.

When I returned to the hotel after the meal, Abu Faisal came and told me that the 'Old Man' wanted to speak to my cousin Mounir.

'Mounir is here in Tunis?' I asked in surprise. 'I'd love to see him again.'

Arafat had already mentioned Mounir to me, saying, 'This cousin of yours doesn't believe in our strategy. He wants us all to become devout Muslims and start a *jihad*, with 10 million Muslims marching on Israel.'

'You don't really mean to tell me that Mounir has become one of those?' I asked.

'I hope you will meet him and see for yourself,' he replied. But I still had not realized that Mounir was actually in Tunis.

Mounir is a second cousin who had been imprisoned in Jordan for his communist beliefs. He was in prison for eight or nine years. I was in Jerusalem for Christmas when they released him in 1965 and I still remember people carrying him on their shoulders, shouting slogans. Since then he had been living in Beirut. There he continued his education at the American University and later joined the PLO, working for the Palestinian Research Centre in Beirut.

'Listen,' I said, when we met, 'I understand that the Chairman is not happy. He says you believe the only alternative is to lead 10 million Muslims in a *jihad*-style war against Israel.'

Mounir laughed, but he said, 'Perhaps it is the only way.'

'Am I to understand that you want to convert to Islam?'

'No, not really.'

He invited me home to meet his wife, a Maronite Christian from Lebanon, and his two children. He lived simply, and I marvelled that he had no one to guard his house.

'But you're a wanted man,' I said.

Mounir and I are about the same age and had become friends when he used to visit Nazareth as a boy. He talked now of his life in Tunis. The simplicity of his lifestyle was a matter of principle. He spoke with disappointment about how some of the leadership lived. 'This is the richest revolution in the world,' he said sadly.

The next morning, before flying home, we were taken to another hotel in Tunis, where we came face to face with the Palestinian writer Raymonda Tawwil, a cousin of my brother-in-law. 'What are you doing here?' I asked.

'I might ask you the same thing,' she replied.

I was surprised to discover that she was so close to the Palestinian leadership. Since then she has become Arafat's mother-in-law!

When we arrived in Rome we called members of the PLP and told them what had happened. Until then no one except our immediate families had known where we were. It was decided to hold a press conference at Tel Aviv airport. We left the building to find a hundred or more journalists waiting, but unfortunately two busloads of *Kach* supporters were waiting for us too. (Kach is the nationalist party led by the late American Rabbi Meir Kahane, which openly calls for driving the Arabs out of the 'Land of the Jews'. It was a member of Kach who shot and killed 27 Palestinians during Friday prayers in the mosque in Hebron in February 1994.) They proceeded to heckle us and pelt us with stones. It was impossible to give interviews under these circumstances, which the police were apparently unble to control. So we split up and Muhammad Miari, Kamel Daher and I went back to Haifa and Nazareth, where we were able to give members of the Progressive Movement messages of encouragement and solidarity from Tunis.

The leaders of the PLO had shown great appreciation of what we had achieved politically inside Israel.

* * *

In early June 1986 my wife and I were in Holland visiting our niece Nariman, who was studying in Tilburg. We took the opportunity to visit an acquaintance in the Hague, where we met Ghazi Khoury again. As we were dining (it was the Muslim feast of Eid Al Fitr, which celebrates the breaking of the fast after the month of Ramadan) the telephone rang. Our friend spoke for a while and then said to me, 'Someone wants to speak to you,' holding out the receiver. I thought maybe it was Nariman, who knew where I was, but to my surprise it was a man speaking, a voice I recognized instantly. It was in fact Chairman Arafat himself, calling from Tunis!

I admit I was speechless for a moment. In Arabic I wished him 'happy feast day', then I lost my voice but he said, 'How are you, *Abuna*?' (*Abuna* means 'our father' and is the Arabic form of address for a priest.)

'Well,' I replied, 'I only wish I could greet you face to face.'

'If you mean that,' he said, 'why not come and see me? Come now and visit.'

'There is nothing I would like more, but I have a problem, my wife is with me.'

'So let me have a word with your wife.'

So I told Suad someone wanted to speak to her, and she came to the telephone, very curious to know who I was talking to. Abu Amar told her she was invited to visit and to encourage me to come. I could not at first believe he was serious, but he insisted, saying, 'After all, you are in Holland and it's been nearly a year since we met.' Then he spoke to our host again and in no time we were booked on a flight to Tunis, leaving the next morning.

We were at the KLM counter of Schiphol airport at 8 o'clock, as instructed. We had been told someone would contact us at five past eight. We waited and waited. It was by now 8.30 and the flight was due to leave at ten to nine. I began to feel foolish and said to my wife, 'Maybe it was just a hoax, someone having a joke at our expense.'

We wondered whether to simply leave quietly. Then we wondered whether we were at the wrong counter and began to panic. Suddenly, only seven minutes before take-off, someone touched my shoulder and asked if I was Riah Abu El-Assal. When I said I was, he said, 'Come on, follow me.'

So the two of us ran after him, hoping that we'd got the right person. In fact he was from the Dutch security service. He pushed us into a bullet-proof car in which Ghazi was already seated, and we drove off across the tarmac with the siren screaming. We raced to gate 35, where our plane was just taxiing towards the runway. The driver got on to his telephone and contacted the pilot, steps were lowered from the plane and in no time we found ourselves in our seats in the first class cabin, being treated like VIPs. The flight captain apologized to the other passengers for the delay, saying that distinguished guests had arrived only now. We had shown no passports and we saw no tickets, but there we were anyway.

In Geneva, where we had to change planes, we were taken to the VIP lounge. Suad and I sat and gazed at each other. We couldn't stop laughing and were still not sure whether to believe what was happening to us. On our arrival in Tunis everyone else disembarked first and again steps were lowered for us. We descended to find three cars waiting for us. We were seated in the middle car and the cavalcade moved off towards the airport building. There we were taken to the room used by the president of Tunisia. We were given lemonade to drink and later driven in the same car to the Tunis Hilton. I told Suad I needed a cold shower. I still thought I might be dreaming!

While I was under the shower, the telephone rang. It was Abu Amar, asking where we were. He said, 'I'm waiting for you, I haven't had my lunch yet. The food is ready, the table is set.'

'Listen,' I said, 'I'm taking a cold shower before I believe any of this is really happening.'

'Right,' he said, 'but hurry up. I'm waiting for you.'

So again the three cars came, and we were taken to our host, who welcomed us with hugs of real affection. By then it was about 2.30 in the afternoon and we ate and chatted, then we left the table and Arafat again peeled sweet oranges for us, or offered us apricots. I could see by my wife's eyes that she could hardly believe that this leader of a nation was peeling fruit for his guests, serving us, joking with us. I recall his mentioning Emile Habiby, referring to him as Suad's uncle. Again I was astonished that he should know and remember so much about us. Arafat said, 'Tell him that the whispers in his house are heard even here in Tunis.' This was a reference to the way the Israeli Communist Party attacked the PLO in their newspaper, the *Ittihad*, and Emile's role in this.

Suad had her camera with her and she asked Abu Amar whether she could take a photo of him in his army cap.

'Oh, certainly,' he said, 'but allow me first to put on my kaffiyah.' He went and put on his kaffiyah, then brought his cap back with him and, laughing, placed it on Suad's head. I took a photograph of the two of them. Another one was taken of the three of us together, Suad, Abu Amar and myself, which now stands on the bookshelf behind my desk.

So we sat for two and a half hours, eating and chatting, and of course exchanging views on the prospects for peace. At one point Arafat asked me, 'What ideas do you have?'

'What spontaneously comes to mind,' I answered, 'is the matter of dialogue. For example, why don't you invite five Israeli musicians, to sit with five Palestinian musicians, say in Vienna. Let them sit there for two weeks, and perhaps they'll come up with an anthem for peace.'

He loved it. He said, 'Go and do it, whatever the expense.'

I carried this story back with me, but two months after we reported that we had been to see Yassir Arafat, the Israeli Parliament passed the law making contact with the PLO an offence punishable by imprisonment.

After a while Arafat suggested that Suad might like to see something of Tunis, since she had never been there before. We were taken on a very interesting tour, after which we returned to the Hilton, where we met other Palestinians. One of them, Hael Fahoum, was originally from Nazareth, and we were able to give him news of his family. We also discussed the struggle of Palestinians in Israel for equal rights.

At 11 o'clock in the evening the phone rang again in our hotel room, and we were invited back for another meeting with the Chairman, which went on until three o'clock in the morning. As we left the basement room I thought we must be the last people to see him that day, but he assured us we were among the first. As he came with us to the entrance to say goodbye, I noticed maybe 25 people of all different nationalities, Arabs and Europeans, Americans, Australians, Africans, all waiting to speak to him.

'Good heavens, when do you sleep?' I asked.

'Some nights I don't sleep at all,' came the reply.

As we left my wife asked Abu Amar whether he had a message for the people at home.

'Yes,' he said, 'I would ask you to kiss all the children of our land.'

She said, 'You mean *all* the children?'

'*All* the children,' he said.

'Jewish and Arab?'

'*All* the children. Give them a hug from me.'

So I asked, 'What about me, do you have anything you would like me to do?'

'Yes,' he answered, 'when you reach home, kneel down and kiss the earth of that land which is dear to my heart.'

We shook hands and hugged, and again as we parted he said, 'Promise also to pray for me.'

twelve *Vatican and Lebanon*

In 1965 I received a permit to go to Bethlehem for Christmas, and arranged with my brother Rohi that we should meet there. It was the first time I had seen my brother since I had left Lebanon 16 years before and it was a very emotional meeting. We recognized each other immediately – which was not difficult as we are so alike people sometimes thought we were twins.

Rohi was obviously doing well. He had supported me during my studies in India. Now he came from Beirut in his own car (while I still did not have the means to buy even a bicycle). We talked non-stop – about the family, our lives, our ambitions and about how we could meet again and prevent borders from separating us. We pledged to meet once a year if possible, but at least every two years, either in Jerusalem or Cyprus.

Our lifestyles were very different. Rohi was alone in Beirut, without family and without ties to the Church, which had disappointed him. I told him how happy I was to be back with the family after our separation during my studies and about my calling. We prayed together. Rohi and I kept our pledge and met regularly after this reunion. Usually we met in Cyprus. Rohi had become an excellent businessman and had so much money he hardly knew what to do with it. Every now and then he would fly to Cyprus, or maybe Italy, and phone to say, 'I'm here, why don't you bring Mum and Dad and join me?'

Every time we saw each other I asked him when he was going to get married. He reached his late twenties and early thirties without showing any inclination to settle down. He would tell me he was happy with his life as it was. He had girlfriends, but none were permanent.

'You need a family: you need children,' I told him. 'Who is going to take over your business otherwise?'

'Everything is taken care of,' he said. 'I know we are all mortal. I have left a will with the local church. Everything I own will go to Hanna.'

At first I thought he meant our father, but soon realized he was speaking of my son. When Hanna was born Rohi invited us all to Cyprus and declared he would take care of all Hanna's needs.

'You just go on having children,' he said. 'I'll look after them.'

He even registered his business not in his own name but in the name of Hanna Abu El-Assal and Sons, to include all of us. In his opinion I had done enough for the family, by fighting for the house and taking care of my mother and brothers and sisters until my father came back. Now it was his turn.

I did not stop hoping he would marry and have children of his own. Finally, at the age of thirty-three he capitulated and agreed he would marry if we could find him a girl from home. 'But that is impossible,' I said. 'How can a Palestinian girl with an Israeli passport come to Lebanon? Why don't you find a Lebanese girl?' Rohi insisted that only a girl from the homeland would do. 'All right,' I said, 'if it is God's will, it will be arranged.'

In 1972 I led a youth group on a trip to Cyprus, where Rohi joined us for some of the time. There were a number of young girls in the group, among them Suad's younger sister, Hala. Rohi, it must be admitted, expressed no particular interest in her, but I persuaded him that if he married her it would strengthen the family ties, and Hala was an educated girl, already a teacher by profession. I always thought of the future, and hoped that our children would remain close. If the wives of the four brothers were to have different backgrounds, there might be some conflict amongst them which would affect the relationship between the families. Rohi agreed, and we discussed the practical problems. Rohi was convinced that once they were married, he would be able to take his wife to Lebanon on his passport.

In 1973, while visiting my wife's relatives in Haifa, we received a phone call from Nazareth. 'Come at once,' we heard, 'Rohi is here.'

Not knowing whether to believe it, we hurried back to Nazareth, and there he was. Rohi had flown from Beirut to Amman, bought a Jordanian passport, crossed the Allenby Bridge, taken one taxi to Jerusalem and another from there to Nazareth – and now he stood before us, large as life and very pleased with himself. We celebrated by arranging his engagement.

'Now that you know the way,' I told him, 'we expect you to come again.'

'Certainly,' he said, and he did. So we arranged his wedding, which was held in Christ Church, Nazareth, on 26 January 1974. Rohi stayed for a few days after his wedding and then left via Jordan to Cyprus, while his bride flew straight to Cyprus to join him.

Very soon an urgent call came. 'Riah, the people who were going to arrange for Hala to come to Lebanon have let us down. She can't get an entry visa. It's very embarrassing. Her uncles have come from Lebanon especially to greet her, Emile Habiby is with her, and they want to know what's going on. What shall I do?' I, too, was in a very embarrassing position. I had encouraged the marriage, I had officiated at the wedding, and now there was talk of an annulment if there was no way of getting the bride to Lebanon. When I arrived in Cyprus the atmosphere was not a happy one. I rushed around, going to all the places Rohi had already visited, with no better luck. Then I tried all the church connections I knew, but with no better success, until someone suggested I try the Papal Delegate.

At my wits' end I called the Vatican Embassy and asked for an appointment. My brother and I entered the office of the Papal Delegate and to my surprise he recognized me. It ensued that we had sat next to each other at the banquet after the dedication of the Church of the Annunciation in 1968. He had worn the habit of a Franciscan monk and I must admit I could not remember him – but I did remember telling some jokes which I might not have told had I realized who was sitting next to me.

I explained the situation to him. 'Do you have your sister-in-law's photograph with you?' he asked.

'Yes,' I replied, a little surprised. I handed it to him. He left the room, returning a little while later with a Vatican *laissez-passer* made out in my sister-in-law's name. 'Do you mean she can travel to Beirut on this?' I asked. He nodded.

'Do you have any more of them?'

'Would you like to visit Beirut?' he asked. 'Do you have a photograph with you?'

I gave him one, and he left the room again, to return with a *laissez-passer* for me. My brother could not believe his eyes. I did not quite trust my own, to be honest.

'Do you mean to say we can go to Lebanon with these?' I asked.

'This very day, if you want to,' he replied. 'All you need is a visa from the Embassy.' He called the Lebanese Embassy in Nicosia and said, 'I'm sending two Vatican citizens, please treat them with respect and give them a visa.'

We went back to tell Emile Habiby, then we went straight to the Lebanese Embassy, where we had already spent so many hours that week. We were all a little nervous of the reaction that awaited us, but as we entered we were greeted with '*Ahlan waSahlan, ya muhtarram!*': welcome, respected one. We filled in the forms, paid a few Lebanese pounds and came out with the entry visa, which I still have today.

As we came out the Consul, a Druze, asked us when we intended to leave for the Lebanon. I did not know. As far as I was concerned we could leave immediately. The Consul suggested we travel with him the next day. So it was agreed. He booked our tickets for us, flying Middle East Airlines, the Lebanese airline. My brother left ahead of us to arrange for our reception in Beirut. The next day Hala and I took a cab, accompanied by Emile Habiby, and Emile's brother and his wife, who were to travel to Beirut the same day. 'What I wouldn't give to come with you, you lucky devil,' Emile said.

I sat in the plane, wondering what lay ahead of us, and twenty minutes later we were circling Beirut, a beautiful city in a beautiful setting, between the Mediterranean and the mountains. As the plane taxied to a halt, a lady in uniform entered. At first I took her for a policewoman. She called my name. I hesitated, uneasy. Then she called 'Mrs Rohi Abu El-Assal' and I could see that she had two huge bouquets with her, to welcome us. Her uniform, it turned out, was that of the Egyptian airline. A royal welcome awaited us. We were escorted from the plane to a waiting limousine, our baggage was taken care of for us. On the runway we saw my brother with Revd Samir Kafity, who later became the Anglican Bishop in Jerusalem. In the waiting cars were my aunt and uncle and a number of other people. No one checked our bags or our *laissez-passers*.

On my first day in Beirut I was fascinated by the car number plates. There were cars from Saudi Arabia, from Qatar, from Syria and Iraq. This was what convinced me I was really in the Arab world. That night we were invited to the Yeldezlar restaurant. I could not believe my eyes. The people! The surroundings! The cleanliness! The service! I had never seen anything like it. Over forty people joined us for a dinner party which went on until one o'clock. Then I suggested we go to bed, since we were all understandably tired, but my brother said 'no sleeping', so we went to the Casino Liban, and at five o'clock in the morning he took us for a 'special breakfast' to Jounieh, a port to the north of Beirut. And so it went on, day after day, for 16 days. It was then I decided that if my turn ever came for a sabbatical, I would like to spend it in Beirut. Some months later, I was back again. I had been to the Vatican Embassy in Jerusalem, presented my *laissez-passer* and requested a *laissez-passer* for my wife and children. I received the same treatment. They asked for photographs of Suad, Hanna and (my family had grown in the meantime) my daughters Lorraine and Rania. Each received a *laissez-passer*. In October 1974 we crossed the Jordan river via the Allenby Bridge and continued to Beirut for my sabbatical.

Beirut

Both my wife and I have strong ties with Lebanon. My brother, as I said, stayed in Beirut when my father returned. Suad's family was originally Lebanese. Her father had come with his own father to Nazareth in the 1920s or 1930s from Marjayoun in Southern Lebanon, and when we went to Lebanon in 1974 we found their names still on the register there. Suad could have taken Lebanese citizenship and our children and I could have become Lebanese citizens through her. This is typical of many Christian families who came from Lebanon to Palestine, where there were better opportunities to find work before 1948. Many came to work as servants in Palestinian homes – ironical when we consider that after 1948 many Palestinian refugees were grateful to find work as servants in Lebanese homes. Before 1948 my aunt had a maid from Lebanon to help her because she went out to work as a midwife. Many, though not all, of those who came were Christians. Some of those from the Orthodox and the Evangelical traditions came because they did not feel secure in Lebanon. Suad's father settled in Haifa.

I decided to study for my MA in Islamics in Beirut. I enrolled both at the Near East School of Theology and at the American University in Beirut, where I began work on my thesis for a master's degree on the relations between Arabs and Jews in the Classical period, from the seventh to the thirteenth century AD, and up to the present day. My studies brought me into contact with several of the American missionaries in Beirut. One day one of them asked me where I came from. 'From Israel,' I answered.

'Oh, would you teach me Hebrew?' he asked.

'Why do you want to learn Hebrew?' I wanted to know.

'Because you people will be coming here,' he replied.

'Who? What people?'

'You Israelis.'

I started to wonder whether some of the missionaries were doing more in Lebanon than preach the Gospel.

My life in Beirut was very different from what I had been used to. My brother took me to his banks and authorized me to use his accounts. To this day my signature is valid in two or three banks in Lebanon. The week we arrived Suad and I were taken to meet a member of the Lebanese parliament, a key figure in the Ministry of the Interior, August Bachus, who welcomed us at the Palace at Baabda. He arranged for us to obtain permanent residence permits for Lebanon.

My brother took wonderful care of us. He enrolled my son, Hanna, in the best school in Lebanon, with a servant to take care of him and a car to take him to his school in the mountains in the morning and bring him home in the afternoon. Others looked after our daughters. Lorraine was already two and a half years old, and Rania a baby of six months. Suad and Hala enrolled for a course in English on Al Hamra, the main boulevard in the Ras

Beirut district of the city. They had servants to help them, so there was little housework for them to do.

The places my brother took me to spoke more of Western than of Eastern culture. At that time Lebanon was still known as the Switzerland of the Middle East. We were invited to the homes of members of the Anglican community, who were among the most affluent in Lebanon. I started noticing that if I asked for a glass of water, my host would call a Samira or a Fatima to bring it for me, and a little girl of nine or ten would appear.

'What is this child doing here?' I asked. 'She should be in school.'

'She is helping in the house,' was the reply. 'We've paid for her for the next three or four years.'

'Where does she come from?'

'From Syria,' or 'She's a Kurd,' or even 'She's a Palestinian refugee,' they said.

I never grew to feel at home in this world. These people were businessmen. I could not compete with them. And although they were very kind to us, hospitable church-goers whom I saw every Sunday in church, I had very little in common with them. They used to talk about their trips to the Caribbean for the fishing, the gold rates, how share prices were doing. Once I said that if I were to stay in Beirut for any length of time, I would lead a demonstration of the child labourers. I would demand the liberation of this generation. One of my hosts turned to me and said, 'You would have not just one, but a hundred guns pointed at you.'

The servants were not just poor Lebanese, Kurds and Palestinians, but came from all over the world, from Sri Lanka, the Philippines, Thailand, Pakistan. There were even offices where they gave you photos of women to choose. Those chosen for their good looks were not only engaged to wait at table.

I made it my business to get to know other areas of Beirut, other ways of living. My brother offered to buy me a car to drive to the university or college. I refused, because I did not think it was in keeping with being a student, and I preferred to use the public transport, the collective taxis which were to be found all over the city. Sometimes I walked part of the way. One day I was standing in the street in Al Bourj, a busy quarter in the centre of Beirut. A friend of mine, Faiz Sakhnini, brother of the Baptist minister in Nazareth, passed me without my noticing. He tapped me on the shoulder and said, 'I've been watching you. You've been standing here for the past hour. Are you waiting for someone?'

'No,' I replied, 'I'm trying to discover the real face of Lebanon. I thought that Lebanon was the Switzerland of the Middle East. It's not true. Come and see, some of these people are in rags, some haven't shaved for days, their children are being exploited as servants.'

While I was back in Nazareth for Christmas I wrote a letter to my brother, which he still has, in which I talked of my fears that this situation could not continue indefinitely, that there would be a social revolution. I certainly did not envisage the civil war which broke out such a short time later. I do not think anyone could have envisaged how quickly Lebanon would break up; or the violence and chaos which would accompany its collapse.

The Lebanese civil war started about three months after we returned to Beirut, although we did not immediately realize what was happening. It was a Sunday, so we went to church in the morning, and in the afternoon took the kids to Jounieh on an outing. On the way back we heard shooting, but took little notice, thinking it was a hunting party. My brother pointed out that it was the pigeon-shooting season. When we arrived home Samir Kafity called from his home in Ras Beirut. 'Riah,' he said, 'Something terrible has happened. You had better take care, you and your family.'

In Ein Roumaneh, the quarter where we were living, a Lebanese Maronite Christian, a member of the Phalangists, had entered a bus full of Palestinians and their Lebanese and Iraqi supporters, and shot dead 30 people before they could overpower him. The passengers were returning from a commemoration event for *fedayeen* killed in a raid on northern Israel.

The next day was quiet, but on the third day the shooting started again. One day shortly after this, I was stopped on my way to the American University by a masked Christian Phalangist, who insisted that I get out of the taxi immediately. He demanded my identity card, but I had left it at home, which was very foolish of me. I should have taken my Vatican *laissez-passer* with me.

Instead I had with me my books on Islam! I did not have my Bible but a copy of the Qur'an. I covered it with my hand.

'Get out!' shouted the masked man.

'Shame on you, speaking to a priest like that,' responded the driver, who had taken me to the college many times before. Unfortunately, that day I was not wearing my clerical garb as I usually did.

'A priest, dressed *en sportive*?' The Phalangist did not want to believe him.

'He lives here, in that building over there,' replied the driver. 'I drive him to his college every day. How do you expect him to cross Beirut dressed as a priest? Should he meet the Muslims in his clerical collar and be shot?'

Luckily, I was spared. The driver assured me that I would have been killed had I got out of the taxi and the man discovered by my accent I was Palestinian – Christian or no Christian. He took me back to the house and refused to take me to the college that day. 'You had better stay at home,' he said.

Things became very bad that week. The shops remained closed and there were no new deliveries. We ran out of milk for the children, and I developed a bad toothache. I decided I would have to go to the pharmacist. I called my aunt in the neighbouring quarter, Furn Al Shubak, to ask if the pharmacy near her house was open.

'Yes, it's open, but you'd better come quickly,' she said.

So I put on my black suit and clerical collar and set out. On the way, just opposite the pharmacy, there was a checkpoint outside the Phalangist headquarters. The headquarters later became the target of a rocket which missed them but blew up the house where my aunt lived, killing her and her eldest daughter. She left a husband and two other young children. Her husband's leg had to be amputated. By chance my mother saw a report on the incident, and thought that she recognized her sister. We told her she was mistaken, and it was not until years later, when another sister died, that we admitted that she had been right, and that her sister was dead. She mourned the two of them together.

I reached the pharmacy safely and bought some painkillers and powdered milk to keep in store for the children. On the way back

I worried that if I stayed on the far side of the road, the Phalangists might mistake my black suit for some sort of uniform, so I decided to walk towards them, say 'bonsoir' as I passed and proceed home. As I stepped off the kerb to cross the road there was an almighty crash as a rocket landed just eight metres behind me. It landed under the balcony of the Cinema Scala, causing the huge lead letters announcing its name to fall to the street below. I was knocked off my feet, and for the moment did not know what was happening. There was a lot of dust. Everyone ran for cover.

A young man lay near me. He had been crossing the road in the opposite direction and was badly hurt, his whole leg covered in blood. Some people came to help me, dragging me into a nearby house. I was not badly hurt although I have retained a scar on my left thumb as a memento of the event. But I did not dare speak Arabic, fearing that my Palestinian accent would give me away. I acted as though I were still under shock – indeed I was shivering badly – and just kept murmuring 'merci, merci'. Someone gave me water to drink and I continued home, to find my brother, Suad and Hanna in panic. They had heard the explosion and called my aunt to know where it was. She told them it was opposite the pharmacy, but she could not see me.

It was enough. I told my brother it was time we were leaving, and on 2 July 1975 we said goodbye to him and his family. We found a driver who knew both sides of the city to take us to the airport. We had no tickets, having been told we would have to buy them at the airport, so we hid the money on the children, in case we were searched. We decided that if I should be picked up, Suad would continue to Jordan and then on to Israel with the children. If we were both picked up, the driver promised to take the children back to my brother. Hanna was now six and a half, Lorraine three and a half, and Rania one year and four months.

We arrived safely at the aiport and after a four-hour wait in a hall crowded with people trying to leave for all parts of the world, we boarded a flight to Amman and home.

In later years I often used my Vatican *laissez-passer* for brief visits to my brother. I flew via Cyprus, where I deposited my Israeli passport at the Israeli embassy for safe-keeping, since it did not seem advisable to have it with me in Lebanon. Thus the Israeli government knew of my visits to the Lebanon. Indeed, I used to bring back little presents for my family, and passed through the airport with them still wrapped in their original Lebanese wrappings, carrying the name and address of the shop where they were bought.

These visits to an 'enemy' country in the years when it was the main base of the PLO never led to any reprisals, and yet my visit to the United Kingdom in 1986 to a conference was deemed to have endangered the State of Israel. Strange indeed!

thirteen *A prisoner in my own country*

Or: Around Israel in 1,249 days

My activities gained a form of recognition from the Israeli government, although admittedly not the kind I had hoped for. On 1 August 1986, two days before I was to leave on another visit to Holland (this time purely as a family holiday), two men walked into the church grounds as I was talking to one of my staff. They asked me in Hebrew where they could find the priest, Riah Abu El-Assal. Something told me they were not bringing good news. I asked them what they wanted him for. After some hesitation they said they had a message from the Ministry of the Interior for him. I introduced myself and received an order, signed by the Minister, Rabbi Yitzhak Peretz, forbidding me to leave the country for the period of one year. It was dated 31 July 1986. To make sure I understood they made me sign the order.

Since the establishment of the State of Israel, travel bans had been issued only six times – and one of these was against my friend and party colleague Kamel Daher. The legal basis for the order was Regulation 6 of the Emergency Regulations (Foreign Travel) (Amendment) Law, 5721–1961. Ironically, this law was introduced by the British during the Mandate and was used against both Arabs and Jews. Many leading Zionists opposed the Emergency Regulations bitterly. Former Israeli Justice Minister and Attorney General Ya'acob Shapira claimed the laws were harsher than those enacted in Nazi Germany. The first Israeli Knesset declared them to be 'incompatible with the principles of a democratic state' and the 1946 Hebrew Lawyers' Union Conference called them 'official terrorism' and 'a serious danger to individual freedom'. None of this has stopped the Israeli government using them, either in the Occupied Territories or in their own country.

The Minister claimed that my projected travels might harm the security of the State, although he did not say why. This made it very difficult for me to disprove the charge. Fortunately, many people have heard me speak abroad and know what I stand for. I appealed to them for support. One of the most marvellous experiences of my life – I think *the* most wonderful – was the way my friends in the country and particularly abroad rallied round me in my hour of need.

I wrote to friends in the Church, those I had met on my travels or while they were in Nazareth, and they rallied to my support. On 25 September 1986 the Episcopal Church's House of Bishops in the United States, under Presiding Bishop Edmond Browning, passed a resolution[1] on my behalf and, to my even greater delight, addressed for the first time directly the question of a Palestinian homeland. They passed a resolution calling for a Palestinian homeland to be established alongside the State of Israel.

Some of the strongest support for my case in the United States came from my American Jewish friends, one of whom quoted the venerable Rabbi Hillel to me: 'What is hateful to thyself, do not to thy neighbour. This is the essential teaching of Torah. All the rest is commentary.' This advice I have not forgotten.

Many people shared with me their reasons for supporting my case, and many of them were very touching. One lady from Wales wrote, 'I am Jewish myself and my parents were killed in Auschwitz and I feel it is my duty to their memory that peace must reign in Israel between the Jewish and the Arab people – otherwise I feel they and the 6 million other Jews died in vain . . .'

Many, many American friends wrote on my behalf to their representatives in Congress and the Senate. Through the Tel Aviv embassy the government of the United States asked the Israeli government to let me travel or to charge me in a court of law. The Israeli Embassy in Washington replied claiming that I intended to use my travels to channel funds into Israel for the use of 'West Bank terrorists', a claim which would be laughable if it were not so serious.

Such accusations made me afraid for myself and especially for my family, since they left us open to attack from any radical elements which chose to believe them. And indeed, in September events did take a very frightening turn. Suad was in our bedroom, changing her clothes after work one day, when a masked gunman suddenly appeared from the balcony and put a gun to her head. He warned her not to make a sound but she was so afraid that one of the children or I might suddenly come in that she ran screaming into the kitchen. The gunman fled, jumping down from a very high wall at the back of the house and tearing his trousers as he did so.

Suad called me and we called the police, who seemed to be in no hurry to investigate, however. They arrived some hours later and did nothing, taking neither fingerprints nor statements. Later we heard that the following morning a group of men stormed the house of Kamel Daher, tearing it apart and claiming to be looking for 'weapons and foreign currency', a preposterous claim against this gentle pacifist.

To me it appears obvious that the two incidents were connected and related to the charges that we were channelling funds. I believe someone intended to plant 'weapons and foreign currency' in my house. Already during the 1984 election campaign my sister-in-law had found a new revolver and a quantity of ammunition on our doorstep. My wife handled it carefully to avoid disturbing fingerprints and reported the incident to the police. As after the later incident, we heard no more from them. Again, no one took statements or fingerprints.

The most exasperating aspect of the whole affair of the travel ban was that no specific charges were made against me. The Attorney General, Joseph Harish, did reply to the various individuals, organizations and embassies who wrote to him on my behalf. In his reply he accused me of having contacts with the PLO and raising funds for PLO purposes in Israel and the Occupied Territories. After giving a brief résumé of the goals and intentions of the PLO as he saw them, he informed enquirers that I could appeal to the Supreme Court of Israel in Jerusalem, and if I was able to refute the evidence against me, I should enter a petition to this Court. He added that I had not done so – implying that this

was suspicious. But I never found out what this 'evidence' was supposed to be.

Later the 'evidence' degenerated to a 'suspicion'. A representative of the Israeli Embassy in Washington wrote to the United
States Congress:

> The facts of the case are as follows:
> The Minister of the Interior, acting under the Defence
> (Emergency) Regulations, has issued an order barring Rev. Riah
> Abu-Assal's departure from Israel for one year, until the end of
> July 1987.
> This order was issued for reasons of national security. There is
> solid and plausible suspicion that his leaving Israel for travel
> abroad could harm the security of the State, specifically since its
> purpose would be to maintain contacts with senior personnel of
> the so-called PLO, with the intention of transferring sums of
> money from that organisation into Israel for subversive purposes
> that no country, no matter how democratic, would or could
> sanction.

I was left wondering how a suspicion can be 'solid and plausible'.

In my own defence I should mention that shortly after the travel
ban was issued, the State Comptroller audited the books of both
the Progressive Movement and the PLP, and pronounced that all
monies received by them were accounted for to his complete satisfaction. Any money I received from abroad came from church
funds or recognized charities. It was not smuggled but declared
openly and used for the purposes specified by the donor.

Kamel Daher did appeal to the Supreme Court to lift the travel
ban against him. The Court studied his appeal and found: 'It was
legitimate for the respondent [the Minister of the Interior] to con-
clude from the material brought before him . . . that the petitioner's
trips were not for humanitarian purposes but, rather, for purposes
which are incompatible with the security interests of Israel. From
this material it is apparent that we are speaking of monies which
the PLO is interested in smuggling into Israel and that the PLO
is doing so under the guise of innocent organizations. In light of
the PLO's well-known objective of the destruction of the State

of Israel, it follows that there is serious fear that these monies would serve ends injurious to the security of the State.'

The Attorney General went on to say that 'Regulation 6 is very rarely implemented and only in those circumstances when a normal court proceeding would endanger the sources of information.' Kamel Daher was not allowed to know what was in 'the material' nor who provided it, or why he had not been charged with smuggling illegal money on his return from his trips. He was never charged with transferring money to illegal or subversive organizations within Israel, or indeed of having any contact with such organizations. Neither was I.

On 4 March 1987, I was asked to come to the Ministry to discuss my case with Yehushua Kahane, assistant to the Acting Minister of the Interior, Ronnie Milo. I had been invited to Britain to attend a conference of the 'Living Stones', and the then Archbishop of Canterbury, Dr Robert Runcie, had interceded for me with the Israeli Ambassador to the United Kingdom. However, at the very outset of the meeting Kahane rejected my request to travel to Britain and reiterated that it would jeopardize the security of the State of Israel.

Apart from the charge of funnelling illegal money we also discussed previous incidents when the Ministry for Religious Affairs had accused me of providing 'inaccurate information' about Israel to the foreign press while travelling abroad. The Ministry for Religious Affairs had already told me after my tour of Australia that my remarks had been monitored and that the Ministry 'had enough evidence to take me to court'; that I had 'harmed the State' by claiming that there are 3,000 classrooms lacking in the Arab sector. I still maintain there were.

I rather suspected this was actually the 'harm' the State feared from me now. I believe that the meeting was probably arranged to give some impression of 'fairness' for the benefit of Dr Runcie and others. It was most revealing that Mr Kahane, and we must assume the Minister, believed that international Christian institutions and organizations supporting economic development and social service programmes in the Arab sector in Israel and the Occupied Territories are channelling funds for the PLO and consciously serving purposes of 'terrorism and subversion'.

In June 1987 a representative of the US Embassy came to see me and told me of their efforts on my behalf. Representatives from the Embassy had spoken to the Ministry of Justice, the Ministry of the Interior, the Prime Minister's Office and the Office of the Foreign Minister. They had obtained a promise that Prime Minister Shamir himself would reconsider my case. I did eventually receive two messages from Deputy Prime Minister Shimon Peres – an invitation to celebrate the Jewish holiday of Succoth with him and another to dine with President Hertzog at the kibbutz resort of Genosar on the Sea of Galilee!

But another three years passed before I was allowed to leave the country again. Since charges were never brought against me, I cannot prove that the claims of the Israeli government were false.

fourteen *Sulha*

All this is from God, who reconciled us to himself through Christ,
and has given us the ministry of reconciliation. (2 CORINTHIANS 5.18)

One evening in October 1973 I was sitting in the little office which
I had set up in the vestry, waiting for the members of the Pastorate
Committee to assemble for a meeting. They were somewhat late,
but I was not surprised – this is the Orient, after all. We had
agreed to settle one or two points of parish business and then go
together to visit my cousin, where another cousin, who had
recently arrived from Kuwait, was staying.

Many Palestinian refugees left their first country of refuge to
work in Kuwait, where they were welcomed because, in
general, they were better educated than the Kuwaitis. They
worked as doctors and teachers and in the civil administration.
The Palestinians became so influential in Kuwait that some
Kuwaitis became jealous. This was part of the reason for their
harsh treatment and mass deportation after the 1991 Gulf War.
My cousin came via Jordan and the West Bank to Israel –
which was, of course, illegal, but was common practice at the
time.

I was using the time of waiting to work on my sermon and was
completely engrossed in this task when a voice asked me 'Qassis,
what are you doing here? Didn't you hear what happened?' One
of the ladies of the Pastorate Committee had arrived and was
obviously agitated.

'What should I have heard?' I asked.

'The Egyptians have invaded the Sinai and the Syrians are already halfway to Tiberias!'

'You're joking!'

'No, I'm serious.'

So I dropped everything and got in the car and went to my cousin's house. On the way we were stopped by the police and asked to darken our headlamps, because 'there is a war on, you know!' Now I was beginning to believe it. At my cousin's house no one was interested in hearing about Kuwait, all were sitting around the television or listening to the radio, following the news bulletins. Again there was talk of an Arab victory. After 1967 I found it hard to believe what they were telling us, but to be honest, in my heart I wanted to believe it.

We began to joke with my cousin, telling him he would be going home to Kuwait by a completely different route, maybe travelling through Syria! We were instructed by radio to stay indoors and keep off the streets, so the party broke up early and everyone went home. The sky was full of planes, criss-crossing above us, but in the darkness it was impossible to tell whether they were Israeli, Syrian or even Egyptian. The next day Syrian television showed film of road signs in Hebrew and Arabic, indicating that they were on Israeli soil. They showed pictures of burnt-out Israeli tanks, Israeli planes which had been shot down and Israeli soldiers who had been taken captive.

For a few days the news from the Israeli side was chaotic. They were not telling the truth. On the second day of the war military leaders were shown claiming they would break the bones of the Arabs. This was followed immediately by news from the Arab world showing the Israeli armed forces in retreat. It sufficed to show us that the Arab armies were not completely inept, that they were at least able to frighten the Israelis. And – more important for us – while the Egyptians were still advancing, President Sadat announced, 'No more war, now we will make peace. Today we have regained our dignity, today we are not defeated, we are even.'

His call was not heard and – some say with the help of the Americans – the Israelis got behind the Arab defences and defeated both the Egyptians and the Syrians. But Sadat had already made it clear in his speech to the nation that this time he meant peace. I am convinced that in October 1973 we missed an important opportunity for what we Arabs of the Middle East call *sulha*, the achievement of peace through reconciliation and compromise.

Sulha plays an important part in Arab society, which revolves around concepts of honour and shame. When someone is wronged, he looks not so much for the punishment of the perpetrator, but for the restoration of his own honour. The loss of honour means a loss of dignity and standing in the community. Let me explain this. In the private sphere the honour of a man and his household is based on two principles: his own behaviour and that of the members of his family; and his ability to defend his family and his possessions.

The example of the first principle best known perhaps to the West is the honour associated with a man's ability to ensure the chastity of his womenfolk. Sex before marriage and adultery are punishable by death in Middle Eastern societies – and it is the girl or woman's own kin who are responsible for punishing her. It is less well known in the West that a man is equally disgraced if someone steals from him, especially if the robber enters his property, his private sphere. The worst disgrace is to allow harm to come to a member of the family.

In the case of a fatal incident, even when the fatality is the result of an accident, the most urgent need is to separate the two parties involved. The person responsible for the incident must leave the community so that his presence does not provoke some impetuous act of vengeance. Normally the police intervene and lock him up for his own protection. Of course the case is taken to court and sentence passed according to the law. But this does not satisfy the aggrieved family. Immediately the death becomes known, a constant stream of people visit the bereaved family and mourn with them. They try to console the relatives, perhaps saying that this was preordained. Muslims in particular believe in predestination. The visitors stand between the two parties. Leading figures from the community – bishops, priests (I am often asked to mediate in a *sulha*), sheikhs and high-ranking police officers – stay in the house of mourning day and night to prevent more harm being done and to control possibly hot-headed younger members of the family.

Some of these leaders form a committee which presents itself to the family and offers to mediate. The committee offers the family a sum of money, usually about 10 per cent of the sum they consider adequate compensation. If the family accepts the money this is a sign that they respect the committee and approve its intervention. Next the committee starts deliberating with all the parties involved until a satisfactory solution is found.

Today, as I said, the family of the perpetrator usually offers a sum of money as compensation. The amount is decided by the committee. This money symbolizes a confession of responsibility. If it is accepted, it means the bereaved family is ready for reconciliation. Some families refuse to keep the money, saying that they will not take money for blood, but they take it and give it to a charitable cause to show that they accept the offering and thus put an end to the need for revenge.

In former times everyone in the community, maybe thousands of people, were involved in such a *sulha*. When the negotiations were complete, the mukhtar of the village and all the community assembled at the house of the victim's family. A procession approached: the perpetrator's family, walking one behind the other. They carried a white flag and led the guilty person on one side and an animal, usually a sheep, on the other. They would stop before the assembled dignitaries. Then one of the dignitaries would say a few words and tie a knot. This would be repeated seven times – seven signifying completeness, in this case that reconciliation between the conflicting parties will be complete. The head of the family presented the one who caused the harm, saying, 'Here is your son – choose between your son and the animal.' Then the animal was slaughtered, a feast was held and the two families broke bread together. Everyone expressed appreciation of the responsible way in which the family of the perpetrator had acted and they could return to their home without fearing revenge.

It can take many years before a satisfactory reconciliation is achieved, and it takes the efforts of many neutral mediators who enjoy the respect of both parties, plus the goodwill of the parties to the conflict. I mention all this because I believe it has a bearing on the peace process in the Middle East. The Palestinians have been invaded; many even killed. They have lost their land and with it their honour and dignity, and until these have been restored there cannot be peace.

Just after the 1967 Six Day War, the President of Israel, Zalman Shazar, came to Nazareth at the invitation of Mayor Musa Ktaily. As the leader of a religious community I was among those invited to meet him. I was not to speak to him directly, but I appealed to those close to him to pass on a proposal for peace. I proposed that Shazar take a plane and fly to the Pope in Rome, call on the then Secretary General of the United Nations, U Thant, and the three of them should fly to Khartoum, where a summit meeting of the Arab leaders was being held. There Shazar should say as he said in Nazareth:

'Listen, we beat you, but now we have come to be reconciled.'

I am convinced President Nasser would have been the first to come forward and hug him. The mere presence of this leader of the victorious side would have made it possible for him to do so. Instead it is said that the then Minister of Defence Moshe Dayan put his feet on the table and said, 'I'm waiting for the first Arab leader to come and sign a peace treaty.' Of course no one called – it would have been dishonourable. It is for the victor to show magnanimity and take the first step, not the one who is defeated.

It is my hope that there will soon be a change in the Israeli government which will bring *Sabras* – Jews who were born and grew up in Israel – and more oriental Jews to power. I believe that these people who are part of the Middle East will find it easier to communicate with the Palestinians. We shall speak the same language. I know it will take great courage on the part of the Israelis, but only reconciliation can lead to lasting security and stability in the region.

However, for peace to be possible the Israelis must fully withdraw from the Occupied Territories. Their presence there is a continuing source of shame and provocation to all Arabs. Then Israel must be prepared to admit that it has wronged the Palestinians, irrespective of whether the wrong was justified from the Israeli point of view. The Palestinians' way of life has been destroyed, they have been expelled from their country, their lands have been stolen and their right to represent themselves denied. This wrong must be recognized. And there must be some form of compensation. The right of the Palestinians to compensation is recognized in the United Nations resolutions on Palestine, in particular resolutions 242 and 338.[1]

The *intifada* or uprising which began in 1987 restored some measure of dignity to the Palestinian people and enabled the PLO to recognize formally the right of the State of Israel to exist. In the Progressive List for Peace, the political party which I helped to establish, we saw this as an opening for dialogue between the two peoples – certainly made difficult by the Israeli government's ban on meetings between Israelis and the Palestinian leadership in the PLO.

The intransigence and brutality of the Israeli authorities in dealing with the *intifada* dealt this hope for dialogue a cruel blow. The PLO itself dealt us a further harsh blow when it accepted Saddam Hussein's claim to be fighting for Palestine in the 1991 Gulf War. I still fail to understand how the Palestinian leadership could accept the occupation of another country by force, when they have reason to know that occupation cannot resolve territorial disputes – quite apart from the moral difficulties involved.

The tenuous dialogue between progressive groups of Israelis and Palestinians broke down under the double strain, and our own party lost its credibility in the process. This was a bitter blow for me personally. More importantly, the way has been opened up for extremists on both sides to fill the void left by the lack of dialogue between reasonable people of goodwill on both sides. However, moderates on both sides are aware that neither nationalism based on territorial claims nor religious fundamentalism have anything substantial to offer their followers in this day and age. We need a new concept for living together.

fifteen *'Islam is the alternative'*

I have always believed that peace in the Middle East and security
for the Palestinian and Israeli peoples depend on their mutual
recognition of their national rights. To achieve this recognition I
have struggled and suffered. In spite of the fact that this mutual
recognition has been achieved through the historical handshake
when President Arafat met Prime Minister Rabin on the White
House lawn in Washington, Palestinian national unity seems to
be threatened from an entirely new direction.

In the Holy Land, Muslims and Christians have lived together
for the past 1,400 years. Sixty per cent of the pupils of Christ
Church School are Muslims. Our school day begins with a
service attended by all the children during which we sing Christian
songs and say Christian prayers. Muslim parents know this and
they accept it. They also know that we do not try to convert the
children. We try to share our faith, but not to impose it. As a
child I remember the relationship between the two communities
as a uniquely happy one. Nearly always one of the Muslim
Fahoum family's girls was picked to be Mary in the school nativity
play. The family was blond and blue-eyed, just as we imagined
Mary to be. In fact I never heard this image questioned until the
1960s, when liberation theologians suggested that Jesus might
even have been black.

The Muslim children show a great admiration for the life of
Jesus, for his miracles, his stories. They learn the parables by
heart and recite them. They appreciate the texts of the songs we
sing in church and generally do very well in religious education
classes. We have much greater problems with the different Christian denominations – the Catholics wanting to emphasize their

Catholicism, the Orthodox their Orthodoxy. However, many Christians and Muslims remain ignorant of the tenets of their own faith, although they watch jealously for signs of a lack of respect on the part of the 'others'. I have observed that anyone can take the name of God in vain impunity, but woe betide the Muslim who belittles Jesus, or the Christian who slights Muhammad.

As an Arab I was always fascinated by Arabic poetry and literature, much of which is strongly influenced by Islam, although I was happy to discover how much Arab Christians and Arab Jews have contributed to Arabic literature and Arab thinking through the ages. I was interested to compare Islam and Christianity, to discover where we think alike and where we differ, which is why I decided to make Islamics part of my studies. My thesis was a comparative study of Christian and Muslim mysticism. My research brought me into contact with many Muslims and I was impressed by the honesty with which people admitted that they had not chosen to be Muslims, any more than most Christians choose to be Christians. They are Muslims because they were born into a Muslim family and brought up in that faith.

Christianity as it reached Arabia was a mixture of heresies. It preached not the Trinity, but a triad – God Father, God Mother and God Son. The Prophet Muhammad challenged this idea and made his central message '*la illah il-Allah*': there is no god but God. Muhammad's God is not a different deity; the Muslim God is the God of Abraham, of Moses, of Jesus – and of Muhammad, whose first and much-loved wife was a Christian.

As the words of the Prophet became better known, many Arab Christians joined the new faith, which they probably did not look on as new, but rather as a clarification of their own faith. My studies taught me that Islam supports our faith in nearly every doctrine. The main difference is that, like Judaism, it is a religion strictly structured by laws, emphasizing submission to a code of behaviour governing daily life. Islam had the advantage that its teachings were in Arabic, whereas the leaders of the Christian churches in the seventh century were foreigners, Greek-speaking Byzantines and others. Hellenistic thinking, Aramaic thinking, Roman thinking and Judaism influenced those Arabs who had been converted to Christianity. This influence came through reading the Scriptures and repeating the liturgies, and led to Arab Christians adopting foreign customs and habits such as giving their sons and daughters Christian names, which were originally Hellenic and later Westernized. Some of them became part of an imperial system which looked down on the local Arabs. Colonialism does not occupy land only, but also infiltrates the spirit and the mind. It shook the confidence of Arab Christians in their own Arab identity. It was no wonder that many Arab Christians welcomed the early Islamic conquests which were, in essence, Arab conquests.

The division of the Church into different denominations as the result of various heresies, each with its own spiritual, if not temporal, army and each with its own customs, most of them far removed from the Arab heritage, have had a similar effect on their Christian identity. I believe it is at least partly because of its disunity that the Church has failed over the centuries to reach the Muslim community. They have seen too many missionaries and too little of Christ. As the Greeks said, 'We wish to see Jesus!' How can they see him today, except through those who claim to follow him?'

Muslims need to see Christ in the Christian layperson, in the Christian clergy and in the church hierarchy. It is unfortunate that many of us do not live in such a manner as to influence the minds of the Muslim community in which we live. In areas of Israel where there is no Christian community, where Muslims are not confronted with our deficiencies and weaknesses, I am met with nothing but respect for Jesus Christ. Muslim friends often ask me for a copy of the New Testament, which I gladly give them. When we speak of discrimination and oppression I share Jesus' message: Love your enemies, bless those who curse you. 'Let us emulate him,' I say. 'If we bless those who bless us, we have done nothing more than is expected. If we curse those who curse us, we have achieved nothing.' My message is well-received and understood.

A number of Qur'an verses speak of Jesus coming to judge the world at the end of days. Like John in his Gospel the Qur'an speaks of him as *kalimat Allah*; the Word of God. The Word which became flesh and dwelt among us. While studying Islamics I asked Muslim scholars if the Word is part of God, if it is therefore divine and eternal. If so, then Jesus is part of the Godhead, part of the Three in One. The Qur'an also speaks of *ruhun minhu*, a Spirit from him. Is this Spirit eternal, is it divine? As I understood my teachers, Muslims deny that Christ was crucified and rose again *because* they believe that he was *kalimat Allah*, he was *ruh Allah*, and therefore could not have died.

I hope that Christians in the world will reconsider their mission to the Muslims. For too long we looked on them as 'infidels', deserving of hellfire, not worthy of salvation; created by a lesser God. No wonder they say, with the great Mahatma Gandhi: 'Take away your Christianity and give us your Christ!'

Because of my interest in the other two religions I am sometimes asked to participate in Jewish, Christian and Muslim trialogues. At one of these I met Sheikh Abdallah Nimr Darwish, leader of the Islamic Movement in Israel. He is a man I respect; frank and honest, a 'graduate of the prisons' as we say, fluent in Hebrew and with a command of Arabic which makes it a joy to listen to him. During my second campaign in the Triangle, for the 1988 general elections, I heard that the leader of the Arab Democratic Party (ADP) had approached Sheikh Darwish to ask him to persuade his followers to vote for them. I went to see the Sheikh and asked him what his position was.

'Come,' he said, 'I'll tell you what happened.'

As we broke bread together, he told me how Abdelwahab Darawshe, the leader of the ADP, had approached him saying that his was a Muslim party, with no Christians on its list. He expected the Islamic Movement and its leaders to support the party.

'In fact,' Darawshe had said, 'we are looking for a sheikh to be on our list. It is time the Muslims had a sheikh in the parliament, to defend their rights, to release the Muslim *waqf* property.'

'I told him,' Sheikh Darwish chuckled, 'we fully expect to have a sheikh in parliament after the next election.'

Nonplussed, Darawshe had asked him if he was thinking of nominating someone.

'No,' replied Sheikh Darwish, 'Canon Riah from Nazareth will be our sheikh. He will speak on our behalf.'

'Well,' I said, 'you have made yourself very plain. Thank you. Now, where do we go from here?'

'We go out on the streets!' he replied. So we linked arms and walked out together on the streets of Kufr Qassem.

That day maybe 50 or 60 young people joined us on the street, asking questions and debating issues; Sheikh Darwish went from home to home asking people to vote for us. This was one of the happiest times of my life – we respected each other, we cooperated for the good of the whole Palestinian people. The leaders of the community had vision and the community itself was behind them all the way. Unfortunately, this blissful state of affairs did not last long. The Islamic Movement in Nazareth won its first victory in the municipal elections of 1988. I went to congratulate the representatives immediately the results of the election were known – at three o'clock in the morning. It seemed only right that I should do so, after the welcome the Muslims had given me, and anyway it seemed important that a member of the Christian community should go to congratulate them. I went to their headquarters near the AsSalaam mosque in the Eastern Quarter of Nazareth.

When I arrived it was as if someone had waved Moses' staff. The crowd parted to let me through and the sheikh welcomed 'our brother the priest'. The crowd started to chant:

Islam wa Mesihiyye
Wahdi Wataniyye
'Muslims and Christians together, one national unity.'

They asked me to say a few words, and after congratulating them I reminded them that our city is holy because it is the home town of the one they, too, revere as the greatest prophet of all. I begged them to use their victory to strengthen Christian/Muslim understanding, not to divide our people.

Next day, as I walked through the *suq* on my way to work, some of my fellow Christians refused to answer my greeting. They would not speak to me because I had gone to congratulate the Muslims on their victory. I believe this is a symptom of the lack of understanding of what is behind the Islamic Movement. The Muslims who voted for the Islamic Movement are not the rich, the affluent and educated, but those from the poorer parts of town, with large families, the ones most subject to discrimination in their daily lives, even in Nazareth itself. It was their way of expressing dissatisfaction with their previous representatives, of voicing their complaint about the sewage that even today flows through the streets of their Quarter, about the roads that are not asphalted, the schools that are overcrowded.

I called one of the Muslim leaders in Nazareth and invited him to my office. I told him of the fear on the part of our community, which drove them to vote for the communist Democratic Front in an attempt to weaken the Islamic Movement. We spoke of the fear and mistrust felt by Christians regarding the growth of the Islamic Movement.

'What do you want me to do?' he asked.

'The Easter festival is approaching,' I said. 'Can you arrange that you and the other sheikhs, the leaders of the Islamic Movement in Nazareth, visit our leaders and wish them a Happy Easter? I am not asking you to come to me. I just want you to make a gesture, to give a sign.' It was not easy for me to ask this. If it had been Christmas, it would have been much easier. The Muslims believe in the immaculate conception and the birth of Jesus. They do not believe in his death and resurrection. So I was overjoyed at the reaction of my visitor.

'It's a great idea,' he said. 'In fact, we will do more than that. You will see.'

At Easter, delegations from the Islamic Movement visited the clergy of each and every Christian denomination in Nazareth, and some of the lay elders of the communities. They brought greetings and offered their services to the Christian institutions in the town. 'We are ready to help with people and money, with all the means at our disposal,' they said. This helped a lot to lessen tension in the town.

Instead, tension grew within the Islamic Movement. Some recognized the need to relate to non-Muslims, some even started talking about a Muslim/Christian party, but the fundamentalists refused to accept this. It is in no way my wish to contribute to the, at times, hysterical fear of an Islamic revival which seems to be the present fashion, not only here, but in the West too. I do not believe that the present extremist representatives of Islam truly represent the needs or wishes of the people. The fundamentalist movements gain popularity because of the services they can provide through the money that is pouring into them from Iran and Saudi Arabia. These include kindergartens and health clinics, as well as cultural centres, especially for the young – services which should be provided by the government. Instead the Israeli government has encouraged the growth of the Islamic movements hoping to weaken Palestinian nationalists. I sincerely believe they will regret this decision, if they do not regret it already.

The Islamic movements seem to offer their adherents something to live for – at times even something to die for. This is a very dangerous development, and one which it will be difficult to contain. Strict adherence to Islamic traditions gives young people a sense of identity. Many of the young girls who have adopted Muslim dress do so against the wishes of their parents (although it is true that others are forced to wear it and rebel against it). The Islamic Movement provides them with places to meet and a sense of purpose. In many Arab countries it finds its followers among the downtrodden and ignored. It takes youngsters who have seen no future for themselves and tells them they are to be servants of God, called to a higher destiny. It gives them a sense of their own value.

In Israel and the Occupied Territories the young are bitter about the lack of progress made by their parents towards peace. They are angry that they are prevented from playing their role in society, unable to fulfil their potential. Many believe that Arab nationalism has failed them. More important still, in the Occupied Territories they feel, with some justification, that they have nothing to lose. This is a very dangerous development indeed.

The bitterness extends to the West, which is perceived as dealing in double standards. Palestinians were bitter to the point of cynicism about the reaction to Saddam Hussein's invasion of Kuwait. This does not imply that they are ignorant of Saddam Hussein's brutality towards his own people. But they do not see why occupation should be despicable in Kuwait and a matter of little interest in Palestine. The treatment of Palestinians after the war, the ruthless expulsion of most of them after they had

worked for years as engineers, teachers, doctors and in the administration to make Kuwait what it has become, while the world
watched with no sense of outrage; the indecisiveness of the
Western powers in dealing with the Yugoslav crisis which mainly
affected Muslims; all these combined to confirm the impression
of ordinary Arabs that they do not count for much in Washington.

Unfortunately for Middle-Eastern Christians, we are perceived
by some Muslims as stooges of the West. The extremists look on
us as enemies, just as they look on the Jews as enemies. I have
heard fundamentalist groups in Palestine say, 'After Saturday [the
Jewish sabbath] comes Sunday' – and my blood runs cold.

But even ignoring such extremes, the Islamic Movement has
taken as its motto 'Islam is the alternative, Islam is the solution.'
For me it is neither the alternative nor the solution, and never can
be. Its gain is my loss, the ruin of all that I stand for and have
struggled for.

So what is the alternative?

sixteen *Bridges to peace*

To refuse to struggle against the evil of the world is to surrender your humanity; to struggle against the evil of the world with the weapons of the evil-doer is to enter into your humanity; to struggle against the evil of the world with the weapons of God is to enter into your divinity. (MAHATMA GANDHI)

When we renovated Christ Church in 1992, a Christian team undertook the stonework, the painting and the woodwork, a Muslim team supplied the windows with crosses in crimson stained-glass, and Jewish teams installed the air-conditioning and created a stained-glass window for the window-frame above the altar, depicting Jesus the Teacher.

I remember telling the Christians in front of the Muslims and Jews that the Christians were meant to be living stones, that more important than beautifying the church building is our presence as living stones. I said how I was reminded of the role of stones in the *intifada*.

I was particularly pleased at the care with which our Muslim friends designed and executed the crosses, since they do not believe in it, they do not believe that Christ was crucified, but that he rose to heaven without dying. I watched them all working together, commenting on each other's work as they went. I joked with the team installing the air-conditioning, saying some of us were certainly hot-blooded, maybe the air-conditioning would help cool tempers a little. Once, when we were all sitting together over a cup of coffee, I expressed my appreciation of their cooperation. I hope we may see it as a symbol of what we can achieve when we work together.

At first some of my parish were unhappy about employing people of other faiths in the church. They suggested I invite monks from Bethlehem to make the stained-glass window, for example. I told them that my decision was intentional. During the few months that the work took, the teams, who were all from Galilee, had a chance to get to know each other, to discuss and debate on all sorts of topics. I myself was pleasantly surprised when I got to know better one of the Jewish men working on the stained-glass window. His family name was Leibovitch, so his father must have come from Eastern Europe originally, but his mother was from Iraq and he spoke fluent Arabic. I was impressed not only by his professionalism and reliability, but also by his understanding of the Middle East.

I was even more surprised when the artist, a Jewess from Russia, approached me after the work was finished and asked me to bless her. I made the sign of the cross on her forehead and gave her my blessing with pleasure.

My vision for the future of Israel is very similar to my experience of our work together in the church. At present I see our people, frustrated and without the freedom to build a new life for themselves out of the ruins of what was. I see the Israelis putting all their energy into trying to suppress another people, instead of using their undeniable talents for the good of their own country. And it will not become any easier. In ten years' time the Palestinians in the Occupied Territories may have reached 4 million. Can 4 million people still be kept under control, caged in, with no hope? How many cars today drive along the Jordan Valley road from the north of Israel to Jerusalem? I always take that route, for the simple reason the road is nearly empty of traffic. Israeli Jews do not travel along it without an armed guard.

The Israeli government claims that it will never let East Jerusalem go; that Jerusalem is the eternal and indivisible capital of the Jewish State. But if you go to East Jerusalem, how many Jews do you find there? A few nervous soldiers and a few arrogant settlers.

I have one son, and I often look at him and think of how I would feel if I had to let him go to the army, perhaps to be exposed to the tensions of serving in the West Bank or Gaza, maybe killing a child and trying to convince himself it was necessary to defend his homeland. How I would feel, going to bed at night, not knowing where he was, if he was safe; not sleeping until he was safely back under my roof. How could I bear it?

I fervently hope that these first tenuous steps towards peace begun in Washington in October 1993 on the White House lawn are the prelude to many more. Autonomy for Jericho and Gaza is not enough. I still believe that Israeli and Palestinian negotiators must agree on a partition of the land which gives the Palestinians a viable state, which I hope will enter into a federation or confederation with Israel. This would still leave open the important question of Palestinian refugees outside the homeland and the question of compensation for private property which has been confiscated or expropriated by the State of Israel.

The Palestinians within Israel have a vital role to play in this process. Until now we have largely been ignored by both the Palestinians outside Israel and the Israeli Jews. And yet we number approximately 750,000: if we take the number of Palestinians in the world to be about 5 million, and the population of Israel is also about 5 million, we make up a sixth of each group. We are a significant minority in both camps and should not be ignored. So how can we help in the search for peace?

Palestinians in Israel should form a lobby. We should work within the Israeli party political system much as the Jews do in America, providing a voice for our people. And – again like the Jews of America – we must provide a voice within Israel both for the Palestinians of Israel and for Diaspora Palestinians. At present all the mainstream Israeli political parties look on themselves as Zionist, but – if we work within them for the good of all Israel – we are strong enough to change their Zionist attitudes and influence our Jewish colleagues to look on Israel as the state of *all* its citizens. We must make ourselves so valuable to the state that no one can question our right to influence the direction of its policies. Arab Palestinian Israelis are numerous enough to influence political thinking in all the parties, with the exception of Jewish nationalist parties.

It is a pity that Prime Minister Rabin made it clear after the general election of 1992 that he would on no account accept an Arab party as part of his coalition government. He was willing, even eager, to come to an arrangement with the Arab members of parliament in which they would guarantee support for his government, but he refused outright to consider including them in his coalition. Sadly he missed yet another opportunity to show the country and the world that Israel respects and accepts its Arab citizens. If we cannot show our brother Palestinians and the rest of the Arab world that it accepts us as equals, how can we expect them to believe that Israel is really ready for peaceful coexistence?

If the Israeli government for its part is serious about its wish for a peaceful settlement, it must act now to protect and support its Palestinian Arab constituents. Peace will eventually mean trade relations with our Arab neighbours. It will mean cooperation on ecological issues of concern to all of us in the region. Palestinians will provide the obvious bridge between the nations. We are present in Jordan, Syria and Lebanon as well as Israel. We have never lost contact with each other, and we understand the systems within which we live. We shall be the obvious go-betweens.

It gave me great pleasure when the first Arab-Israeli ambassador was appointed to take up a mission at an embassy in Scandinavia. I hope that this appointment is symbolic, that it is a recognition of the argument which I have been making for some years now — that Israeli citizens of Palestinian background are the obvious mediators in the Israeli–Palestinian conflict!

It did not surprise me, by the way, that Norway was the venue for the talks that led to the breakthrough in relations between the Palestinians and the Israelis. I have always had warm relations with the Church and the government in Norway, and I know how sympathetic they have always been to our plight. In 1990 I was in Norway for a public debate with the Chief Rabbi of all Scandinavia, Melchior, to which were invited Christians, Jews and Muslims, Israelis and Palestinians. Apart from the openness, fairness and warmth with which the Norwegians offered themselves as mediators, I was impressed by the generosity with which they, again through the good offices of church and government, offered practical support in the form of financial aid for the high school in Nazareth, something we had been fighting for since the mid-1970s. In 1993 we finally received permission from the Israeli government to go ahead with building the school, and I hope it will become a symbol of the Norwegian success in helping the Palestinians to achieve equality in Israel.

In our struggle for equal rights and equal opportunities we shall depend on the world for support for a long time yet. While the Jews were receiving assistance from Jews all over the world, we could not appeal to the Arab nations for support, financial or otherwise. Obviously, this would have been looked on as treachery. But we did not benefit from the aid coming into Israel from the West or Diaspora Jews, so again we were caught in between, belonging neither here nor there.

Israel has been able to prosper because of the aid she has received from the United States of America and the European Community. The United States justifies its massive aid to Israel with the claim that Israel is the only democracy in the region. However, a true democracy does not exclude nearly a fifth of its population from development projects. If the United States is truly concerned to protect Israel as a democracy, it should be concerned to protect democracy in Israel, and this means equal opportunities for its religious and ethnic minorities. Until now, the United States has given Israel a free hand with the aid it receives, with the result that there is little or no development in the Arab sector. I call on the United States and all who invest in Israel to do so for the good of *all* her citizens. Non-Jewish citizens of the State of Israel must be given an equal chance to contribute to and to benefit from their country's development.

In Israel the influence of the state on the economy is very great as a result of Israel's originally socialist structures. We are highly developed technologically, especially in the fields of medicine, communications and military technology. Palestinians have been prevented from entering these fields for 'security reasons'. Much business activity is controlled by cartels and monopolies. Competition in agricultural products such as fruit and vegetables is strictly regulated by a state marketing board, which excludes produce from Arab farmers, preferring to import European fruit and vegetables in times of shortage rather than marketing Arab produce. Israel has traditionally looked to Europe as well as the US, and has a free-trade agreement with the European Union. Some Israelis would even like to see Israel applying for EU membership, or at least associate status, but Israel is not part of Europe (even though it participates in the Eurovision Song Contest) and in the long run will increasingly look for new markets in the Middle East.

There are those who believe – and I hope they will be proved right – that in an era of peace the huge resources of the Arab world will open up to the Palestinians of Israel and they will be preferred in jobs where the function is to act as representatives and mediate between Israel and the Arab world. They will be able to seek work, study and raise money in the Arab world, finding new sources of wealth for the community. This depends to a large extent, of course, on whether the Arab world is interested in trading with Israel and really has wealth to distribute. Others believe the new situation will indeed lead to new prosperity, but it will be exploited by the Ashkenazi who control the economy.

I have said many times to Jewish friends that I hope the soldiers of the army of occupation will soon leave the territories of Palestine to return as partners in business, but there is a danger that opening up its borders to its Arab neighbours could strengthen Israel's need to emphasize its Jewish-Zionist character as a reaction to its exposure to the Arab and Islamic world. Israel may become more Jewish for fear of being assimilated into the region.

If, freed of the need to fight for the rights of our Palestinian brothers and sisters outside Israel, we start to concentrate on the fight for equal treatment in respect of education and job opportunities, will our Jewish compatriots view our demands as threats, which may lead to racial tensions on European lines? The freedom to strengthen ties with Palestinians in the Palestinian homeland will strengthen our Palestinian identity. If the Israelis look on this as a threat it could lead to relations between the Palestinians and Israeli Jews in Israel becoming worse than those between Palestine and Israel. Might Israeli citizens of Palestinian origin not become victims of this reaction? If a Palestinian homeland does come into being, will we be told: 'You have a home of your own now. Go and live in it!' Will our struggle to stay on our land start all over again? And what will happen to security personnel freed of the job of controlling the Occupied Territories? Will they have more time for 'internal security matters'?

Palestinians in Israel are the living proof that Israelis and Palestinians *can* live together in peace. If we are given the chance, we will do our part to make a success of this latest peace venture. I pray that this time, we will be given a chance.

seventeen *An endangered species*

*What frightens me is not oppression by the wicked, it is the
indifference of the good.* (MARTIN LUTHER KING)

When I was in Cyprus in 1976 with a German group from the
Evangelische Student Gemeinde we visited Rauf Denktash, the
Turkish-Cypriot leader. In the course of the meeting I asked him
how he would identify himself first – as a Turk, a Cypriot, a
Muslim...

'You are not German, are you?' he asked.

'No,' I said, 'I am Palestinian.'

'Ah,' he said, 'I did not think a German would ask such a
question.'

A Christian presence

I have often been asked what I consider the most important aspect
of my identity. Until now I have always answered that I define
myself first as a Palestinian, because this is the aspect of my identity
which is threatened. Nowadays I hesitate, because my identity as
a Christian seems to be equally under threat.

In earlier chapters I have tried to show how, as 'non-Jews',
Christians and Muslims alike find it hard to take their rightful
places in Israeli society. My whole life has been dedicated to the
struggle for the recognition of the injustices suffered by the Palestinians as a result of the establishment of the State of Israel. This
is a struggle for the recognition of our national rights, and
neither I nor my colleagues ever thought to discriminate between

Christian and non-Christian Palestinians. Sadly, I now seem to be witnessing the disintegration of our national unity, and the increasing isolation of the Christian community.

Christians, not only in Israel but in the whole of the Middle East, are rapidly becoming an insignificant factor, in terms of both numbers and influence. In Israel we have become so marginal that no party thought it important to have a Christian in a secure place on its list of candidates for the last general election. There is no one in the Knesset to look after Christian interests. Christians who feel they have no voice here are leaving the region. Whole areas of Nazareth which used to be Christian are being given over to Muslims, as the Christian families leave for the West, for the United States, Australia, Canada, where they can bring up their children in a Christian environment and be proud of their origins: where to be a Nazarene is something precious and special.

In a message I gave to His Holiness the Pope at an audience in July 1991, I wrote the following:

Message to His Holiness Pope John Paul II
Firstly I would like to thank Your Holiness for this opportunity to share with you some of our hopes and concerns in the Middle East, in particular those of the Palestinian Arab Christians in the Holy Land. Your Holiness' words to the Extraordinary Vatican Summit of 4/5 March this year, on the exalted mission of the Church in the world and for the world being not of a political character but the desire of the Church to awaken a sense of truth, justice and fraternity, were extremely heartening.

As a minority in our own country we, the Palestinian Arab Christians of the Holy Land, feel a particular need for fraternity, for closeness with our brothers and sisters in Christ. During the recent war [the Gulf War of January/February 1991] we greatly missed the supporting presence of fellow Christians from other countries as a demonstration of solidarity with those of us who have kept the torch of His Word burning for 2000 years in the Land of Our Lord's birth.

Under the pressures of living as a minority with two sister religions, both of which receive massive support from their co-religionists in other countries, the flame is beginning to falter.

More and more Christians, especially the young, are leaving for other countries. Whereas in 1967 there were twenty-eight thousand Christian Arab Palestinians in Jerusalem, today there are closer to seven thousand. In Nazareth, once a predominantly Christian town, Christians now comprise only approximately 35 per cent of the population.

Christian presence is diminishing for many various reasons. Among other things, loss of our land has led to an emphasis on education as a means of self-improvement among Palestinians but educational opportunities for non-Jews in Israel are extremely limited and our young people look to the United States and Europe for higher education. They do not easily return to compete on unequal terms for the professional openings Israel offers. Thus families are split and the brightest and best of our young people are lost to the community.

We recall the words of Pope Paul VI in the Apostolic Exhortation 'Nobis in Animo' (1974) 'Were the presence of Christians in Jerusalem to cease, the shrines would be without the warmth of a living witness and the Christian Holy Places of Jerusalem and the Holy Land would become like museums'. I myself have often spoken to pilgrims of the importance of the 'Living Stones', which bear so much more witness to Christ's message to humanity than shrines and 'Holy Places' ever can.

In the *Osservatore Romano* of June 30–July 1, 1980, the Holy See stated that 'the Vatican does not approve of Israel's taking on itself the task of defending and protecting Christians and Christian interests in the Middle East', a view shared by the Christians of the Middle East, who would like to be the custodians of their own interests but look for encouragement and support to the Christians of the world. The time is ripe for what might be termed a Strategy of Presence.

Like their Jewish counterparts, indigenous Christians who are Israeli citizens have the right of return to their own country and must be encouraged to make use of it.

In this connection an international, interdenominational conference on 'Christian Presence in His Land' is urgently needed.

Furthermore, as Arab Palestinian Christian Israelis we also

have a significant role to play as a bridge in the search for peace and justice for this region. As Christians we are members of the larger Christian community, as Arabs we are part of the Arab world, we belong to the Palestinian nation and we are citizens of the State of Israel. Therefore we feel especially called to serve as mediators in the cause of reconciliation and hope in so doing to reconcile within us the conflicting aspects of our own identity.

Nazareth, 4 July 1991

Pax and Salaam

A Christian's response

In Israel today a Christian minority is living with a Jewish majority. Inevitably, relations between us are burdened by the history of anti-Semitism in the Western churches and discrimination of the Jews in Europe. Unfortunately, Christians in Israel are the victims of misunderstandings arising from the poor relations between Christians and Jews in Europe.

At the General Assembly of the Church of Scotland in 1992, when the topic of partnerships with churches overseas was raised, one of the partnerships announced was that with the Episcopal Church in the Middle East. One of the ministers present, who is an ex-moderator of the Church of Scotland, stood up to protest, saying that the Episcopal Church in the Middle East is anti-Semitic. Now this is obviously not true, because most of the members of the Episcopal Church in the Middle East are Semites. So we need to look at the term and see what it is generally understood to mean.

Anti-Semitic usually refers to anti-Jewish thinking and behaviour in Europe and to a much lesser extent in America or the other 'Western' countries. In the Middle East we do not have a history of 'anti-Semitism' or anti-Jewish attitudes. I was disappointed that a majority in the Assembly seemed willing to believe the charge, without stopping to think that Christian opposition to the Jews in Israel is founded on real experience of discrimination by these people while the Christians are in the minority, and is in no way to be compared with European anti-Semitism.

Many, mainly evangelical, Christians believe that the

establishment of the State of Israel is the first step towards the 'ingathering of the Jews' of prophecy, presaging the Second Coming. They are willing to invest a lot of money to speed up this process. Sadly, they identify with the dreams of the Jews to the exclusion of all others, including their brother and sister Christians in the Middle East, who are Arabs.

Church leaders in the world should, however, consider how their statements can affect Christian minorities. For example, Muslims in the Middle East have reacted very sensitively to statements by the Anglican hierarchy in the West concerning relations with Arab countries; such as the Archbishop of Canterbury's declaration that the 1991 Gulf War was a just war. The Anglican community in the Middle East, often perceived as a Westernized community, is in a particularly vulnerable position.

Although it may sound strange coming from a bishop, I would like to state here that I would prefer to live in a secular state. Faith is a personal matter. I myself strive to live my faith in such a manner that others may, in some way, see Jesus in my life. I do not wish to *impose* my faith on others, any more than I wish to be forced to live according to the laws of other faiths. I do believe that if others, Muslims or Jews, strive to live their faith in a spirit of tolerance and love, we shall all grow closer to God; and this is my prayer. In the meantime, we live in an imperfect world, and I believe that a secular democracy gives us the best chance to live, each according to his or her own beliefs, for the greatest good of all.

However, Christians in the West have a special responsibility at this time, as I have tried to show, towards their fellow Christians in the Middle East. Jews around the world make considerable sacrifices to support their fellow Jews in Israel. The Muslim countries are using their great wealth for the benefit of Muslims in Israel and Palestine. Only the Christian community is not receiving similar moral and practical support. We are perceived as weak, without protection and vulnerable – and in this part of the world, this reflects negatively on the Christian community in general, which loses honour by not protecting its own, quite apart from the fact that the Christian community appears uncaring and therefore unchristian.

Middle Eastern Christians are generally well-educated with high professional qualifications. They are open to new ideas and eager for social and economic progress. They are frustrated on both counts. We cannot progress economically or socially in a country which looks on us as second-class citizens and bars us from work in sensitive areas of the economy. Those who leave first are the educated, the ambitious and talented, who know that in Israel the hurdles they face are too great to be taken. They despair of taking their rightful place in Israeli society. But Christians also have a particular role to play as bridges for peace.

I do not think it is a coincidence that Dr Hanan Ashrawi, spokeswoman for the Palestinian delegation to the Madrid peace process, has made such a strong and positive impression on Western audiences in particular. Dr Ashrawi was brought up in an Anglican family. No one can doubt her sincerity and integrity in her fight for a homeland for her people. She is a Palestinian nationalist. But her education and upbringing made it possible for her to communicate with Western partners. She is an excellent example of what I hope to see Arab Palestinians achieve.

My own plight during the period of the travel ban received much sympathetic attention among Western Christians. The House of Bishops of the United States Episcopal Church not only supported my fight to have the ban repealed, but, as I said in Chapter 13, in consequence of the debate on the subject declared, for the first time, its support of the Palestinian right to self-determination and a state side by side with Israel. I am convinced that my own position as a priest of the Episcopal Church made it much easier for the Episcopal Church in the United States to take a positive stand for the Palestinians.

On a formal and informal level, Christians can do much to promote understanding between East and West. We here have done much, I believe, to make the Holy Land as a cradle of our faith come alive for pilgrims and visitors. Instead of visiting one church, one holy shrine after another, many today look to a meeting with local Christians to enrich their visit and add a new dimension to their faith.

Since the restructuring of the Jerusalem Diocese of the Episcopal Church, the Church in Jerusalem has reached out to many of our Christian brothers and sisters in the world. As Palestinian priests or bishops we can share our concerns in a way that no outsider can. Key figures from the Anglican Communion – Archbishop George Carey, Archbishop Desmond Tutu and the outgoing Bishop of the Episcopal Church in the United States, Edmond Browning, as well as the Presiding Bishop, Frank Griswold, to mention but a few – have responded with sympathy and solidarity.

Inter-church relationships also have a significant role to play in increasing understanding among the parties to the Middle East conflict, and the World Council of Churches provides an important forum for our struggle to be heard in the world. The Episcopal Church in Jerusalem was one of the founder-members of the Near East Council of Churches, formed in the twentieth century, which later became the Middle East Council of Churches, the regional body of the World Council of Churches. It served with sister churches to develop the work of the Council, until today it comprises all Orthodox; Oriental Orthodox; Anglican and other Protestant churches; and Catholic churches in the Middle East. Through the Central Synod the Jerusalem Diocese of the Episcopal Church is represented on the World Council of Churches and continues to support its ecumenical activities.

Like the smaller families in local politics, the Anglican Church as a small community may be able to play a significant role in the ecumenical movement. It is not big enough to be looked on as a rival to the bigger, older established churches. Also, because we are neither Catholic nor wholly Protestant we may be able to provide a bridge between these two branches of the Church. Of course we should not overestimate our own importance, like the first Anglican Bishop in Jerusalem, who wrote in his memoirs that the whole city of Jerusalem came out to greet him on his arrival, with drums and flags. What he never realized was that his arrival happened to coincide with the Muslim holiday of Eid Al Fitr . . .

We should not overestimate our own importance. We have often been accused of arrogance and we should be more careful. Other churches are now educating their clergy and providing leadership for their people. We should not underestimate our own potential, but should serve in a spirit of love and humility.

eighteen *Meet the Nazarene*

'Can anything good come out of Nazareth?'... 'Come and see.' (JOHN 1.46)

My experience at the World Council of Churches conference in Nairobi in 1967 and my contacts with pilgrims to the Holy Land opened my eyes to the fact that few of our brothers and sisters in Christ realized that Nazareth was no longer the sleepy little village that Mary and Joseph knew, but was caught up in a modern-day turmoil that threatened our very existence. It is pitiful to see how few of the pilgrims are aware of the existence of indigenous Christians. In Nazareth there are perhaps a dozen churches, all with lively congregations, in spite of the fact that many of our men are at work on Sundays, in Israeli industries.

Still today groups of people walk up the Casanova, the street leading up to the Church of the Annunciation in Nazareth, to view the place where the Roman Catholics believe the Angel Gabriel appeared to Mary (the Greek Orthodox believe he met her at the well over which their church is built. I personally believe that they probably met at the well and walked back together to her home in the grotto where the Roman Catholic church is now – and I'm sure they paused for a rest just where Christ Church stands today...) but the groups of pilgrims who walk through the crowds on the road leading up to the church, which is close to the *suq* in Nazareth and nearly always busy, look neither to right nor left. If they are aware at all that the people around them are Arabs, it is probably because their Israeli guide has warned them to be careful and guard their valuables. I would not like to hazard a guess as to how many know that the majority of the people around them are fellow Christians who have lived and worshipped in Nazareth since the time of Our Lord. Most of them do not even have the time to stop and buy a postcard from the souvenir shops lining their way, let alone discover that the owners of the souvenir shops are Roman Catholics, Episcopalians and fellow Christians from other churches. What a loss for them, as well as for us.

Talking to a group of pilgrims in the church one day recently, I noticed a man slumped in a pew with his feet up on the one in front of him. I assumed there was something wrong with his leg. I spoke to the group as I normally do, about our life in Nazareth, about our school and its history, about our hopes and concerns. After the talk I shook hands with all the members of the group, until I approached the man who had been sitting with his feet up on the pew. He made it clear that he did not wish to shake hands with me.

'I don't say *shalom* to people like you,' he said.

'I don't understand,' I said. 'What is your name?'

'Why do you want to know my name?'

'I want to go back into the church and pray for you.'

'You're mad!' he said. 'You can't talk to me this way.'

'How do you expect me to talk to you?'

The answer was a very rude gesture. The group he was leading was very angry and embarrassed. They wrote to the Ministry of Tourism and complained, asking for another guide.

But this was not an isolated incident. I have met similar reactions in many guides who do not wish to hear the other side of the story. Sometimes, when we are talking about discrimination, I ask the guide how many of his colleagues are Arabs, and how many of those taking Christian pilgrims around the Christian holy sites are Christians themselves. The answer is usually evasive. I can tell them that there are very few, although there are many Christians who are fluent in at least three languages and would love the work. They would love to take pilgrims to the holy places, to pray with them, to read with them from the Scriptures – and take them to meet local Christians, which is probably why they are not so popular with the government.

In 1968 I could bear it no longer. I initiated a project which I called '*Meet the Nazarene*'. We started to contact tour leaders from abroad and invited them to bring their groups to join us in worship and to meet local Christians. I personally went to all the hotels in town and hung up notices inviting pilgrims to worship with us and to meet local Christians. I left the times of our services and our telephone number, so that people could reach us. Members of the community would invite pilgrims home to taste local dishes and get to know each other over small cups of Arabic coffee. The project was an amazing success. It has undergone changes in the last thirty years, but the idea is still alive, and now maybe a thousand pilgrims a year pass through Christ Church alone, worshipping with us, sharing our hopes and concerns. And always I emphasized the same point, that we wanted people to come. Pilgrims from all over the world visit the Holy Places, and we invited them to meet us when they came.

Everyone is welcome and everyone who begins to understand our situation is important and can make a difference: but I admit I have been pleased when our visitors have included American senators, bishops, parliamentarians from various European countries. I hope that they may be able to influence their own governments to moderate their policies towards us. Sometimes I sat in my office until late in the night, typing and writing replies to the enquiries and letters of sympathy which came from all over the world. My wife did not always appreciate it, when I came home hours late for supper.

One year I invited the ambassadors and staff of all the embassies in Tel Aviv to join us for Palm Sunday worship. Palm Sunday is a big holiday in Nazareth. All the children dress in their new spring clothes and the little girls come to church carrying candles decorated with flowers or ribbons. The church is decked with palm leaves which form a tunnel from the door to the altar. The scout bands and various youth groups parade through the town playing music and carrying palm leaves. Everyone turns out for the occasion. The atmosphere is very festive, and I was sure the embassy people would enjoy it.

I spoke on the destruction of Jerusalem, taking as my text Luke 19.41–4. Many came, and afterwards they told me how interesting it had been to listen and to talk to members of the congregation. The contacts grew – and when I needed support during the travel ban, I was very grateful for the loyalty of these friends, and blessed the inspiration which had made me reach out to them. I have always believed that people cannot be blamed for not knowing if you do not make an effort to tell them.

'How shall they hear without a preacher?'

These visits have been a great source of strength and encouragement for me in my 28 years of ministry here – but I am not easily satisfied. I would like our visitors to spend more than half an hour with us. I would like to see Nazareth become the centre of pilgrimage in Galilee. We have several hostels for pilgrims, including our own St Margaret's Hostel, which offers comfortable accommodation and room for group discussions in an idyllic setting overlooking the plain of Jezreel as far as the Jordan valley. My dream is that we have groups to stay here, to meet and share their faith with us, for the spiritual renewal of both of us.

As a member of the Anglican community I have been able to reach more than usual numbers of supporters. Through our services, especially our hospitals and schools, we have been able to reach many of our own people and serve them. But they have also provided points on which people outside the country and sympathetic to us can focus their help. Our services, which are there for everyone, irrespective of faith or creed, provide also a bridge to the Muslim community and are certainly one reason why my relations with that community have been so happy. Since 1967, when I participated in the conference on education in Nairobi, I became a resource person for the World Council of Churches. Delegations to the Holy Land visited Christ Church on fact-finding missions, and I was asked to provide information on specific questions regarding the situation of indigenous Christians.

I have been invited to participate in conferences and meetings on Christian/Jewish/Muslim discussions organized by the WCC. I became a permanent member of the Human Rights Advisory Group to the Church Commission on International Affairs (CCIA), which brought me in contact with people from many different parts of the world. The Human Rights Advisory Group helped draft resolutions on the situation in Palestine, Lebanon, Cyprus, South Africa and other areas of the world where human rights were being violated.

I was invited to Australia, where we now have a partnership with the Uniting Church, and we have partnerships with the Presbyterian and Methodist Churches in the USA, as well as with our own denomination, the Episcopalians. In America I was also invited to address Jewish groups working for peace, such as American Jews Against Zionism (AJAZ) and the International Jewish Peace Union (IJPU), among whom I found some of our most understanding sympathy and strongest support. Again, when I needed friends during the period of the travel ban, these people rallied round me and gave me great support, lobbying their members of Congress and writing to the Israeli government on my behalf. I shall never forget their care.

Among the groups who visited us were people from all walks of life, including politicians and government officials from Western countries, journalists, activists in peace movements but also many ordinary people who were so moved by what they saw that they were prompted to tell others what is happening in the Holy Land. Some of these have become close and faithful friends.

nineteen *The Good Samaritan*

*'A man was going down from Jerusalem to Jericho, and fell into the
hands of robbers, who stripped him, beat him and went away,
leaving him half dead. Now by chance a priest was going down that
road; and when he saw him, he passed by on the other side. So
likewise a Levite . . . But a Samaritan while travelling came near
him; and when he saw him, he was moved with pity. He went to
him and bandaged his wounds, having poured oil and wine on them.
Then he put him on his own animal, brought him to an inn and
took care of him.'* (LUKE 10.30–4)

I have often found the parable of the Good Samaritan useful in
illustrating our condition. There are many parallels in the suffering
of the man going down to Jericho and that of the Palestinian
people. Three groups of people encounter the man on his
journey: they represent three types we find in the world.

The first say, 'What is yours is mine.' They try to deprive you of
your right to be yourself, of your right to your land, of your
right to education in the field of your choice, your right to equal
job opportunities. After 2,000 years some people came back and
claimed, 'What is yours is mine.' The people living in the land
had nothing to do with what happened 2,000 years ago. We were
not responsible for what happened to the Jews at the hands of the
Romans. We lived here under the Romans, the Greeks, the Ottomans. And then people came and told us: this land is not yours,
these houses are not yours, the water is not yours, the air is not

yours ... We were robbed, and it is very painful to lose one's possessions; one's home and one's country. We were wounded, and our injuries are not only physical but also spiritual, through the denial of our very existence.

Then came those who passed by. In my mind these represent some of the Arab regimes and some Western governments who apply double standards in their dealings with other states; but I also see them in many of those who come to us calling themselves pilgrims. They say, 'What is mine is mine – and I am not going to risk losing it to help you!' I marvel at their selfishness. The Saudi Arabians, the rulers of the Gulf States – they have so much. As the Canaanite woman said to Jesus, 'Even the dogs enjoy the crumbs which fall from the tables of their masters.'

We have been treated for many years like the dogs, forced as refugees to queue for rations, for handouts, for the crumbs which fall from the table. What did the injured man feel, as he lay by the side of the road? Was the indifference of those who passed by not at least as hurtful as the experience of being robbed itself? I have often wondered what the injured man's thoughts were as he lay by the side of the road. Did he cry for help until he could cry no more? When he heard the third person coming, did he determine in his desperation to make sure that this person did not overlook him? Maybe he, too, took up a stone near his hand and threw it. Luckily the Samaritan did not label him a terrorist for his action ...

This is the third type, who says, 'What is mine is yours.' He is not proud. In order to lift up the wounded man, the Samaritan is forced to bow down to him, to pick him up from where he lies in the dust. He does what is necessary and goes on his way. Who made known what had happened? I do not believe that it was the Samaritan. I believe it was the man who was saved, who was healed. He told of his suffering, but also of the restoration of hope. He was trying to tell the world that good will ultimately overcome. The Samaritan acted out of a conviction that the man was worth the life God had given him. He simply helped to heal him; to give him the strength to stand again by himself. When the Palestinian people receive the help they need to stand by themselves again, they will not forget. They will share the experience with others.

There is no mention of revenge in the story, only pain and fear – and courage. The two who passed by were afraid, afraid of suffering the same fate as the man lying in the road. They looked, and ran away. How many in the world look and run away?

We have yet to discover who will be our Good Samaritan. We continue to pray for him – and like the wounded man we may have to wait for a stranger, someone not of our own, to fill the role.

Glossary

Ahlan waSahlan Ar.: Welcome (form of greeting)
Al Ard. Ar.: The Land
Al Fajr Ar.: *The Dawn* (Palestinian newspaper published in Jerusalem)
Al Kutla Al Wataniya Ar.: the 'National Bloc' – forerunner of the
Progressive Movement
Al Sawt Ar.: The Voice (name of an independent publishing house in
Nazareth)
Al Taddamun Ar.: *Solidarity* (name of newspaper published by the
Progressive Movement in Nazareth)
Allahu Akbar Ar.: God is Great – opening of the Muslim call to prayer
Alternativa Heb.: Jewish faction of the Progressive List for Peace
arrack Ar.: strong colourless liquor made of raisins, milky white when
diluted with water, drunk widely in the Middle East
Ashkenazi Heb.: name given to Jews from Eastern Europe
baclawa Ar.: a traditional dessert, very sweet.
chutzpah Yiddish: nerve, gall, cheek
Druze a religious sect living mainly in the mountains of Syria and
Lebanon, branches of which live in northern Israel, especially in the Carmel
mountains
dunum Ar.: measure of land equivalent to quarter of an acre or 900 sq. m.
Fatahland name given to area of southern Lebanon in which the Fatah
group of the PLO, led by Yassir Arafat, was in control.
fatiha Ar.: the opening *sura* of the Qur'an, used by Muslims as a prayer
fedayeen Ar.: fighters, especially those willing to sacrifice their lives for their
country; members of an Arab commando group
Filasteen Arabic for Palestine
hara Ar.: neighbourhood, district (of a town etc.)
HaTikva Heb.: The Hope (title of the Israeli national anthem)
intifada Ar.: lit. 'shaking off', name given to the popular uprising which
broke out in the Occupied Territories in December 1987

155

Ittihad Ar.: *Unity*; name of the Communist Arabic daily newspaper in Israel

jihad Ar.: holy war against the infidels (Muslim religious duty)

Kach name of the nationalist party which calls for expulsion of Arabs from the 'Land of the Jews'

kalimat Allah Ar.: 'the Word of God'

keffiyah Ar.: square of white or black and white chequered cloth worn by Palestinian men as a head-covering

kibbutzim Heb.: plural of 'kibbutz', a collective farm or settlement in Israel cooperatively owned and managed by the members and run on a communal basis

Knesset Heb.: the Israeli parliament

la illah il-Allah Ar.: 'there is no god but God' – article of Muslim faith

laissez-passer travel document, usually issued to those whose nationality is unclear, who are therefore not entitled to a passport

laji'een Ar.: refugees

mabruk Ar.: lit. 'may it be blessed' – term of congratulation and approbation

marhaba Ar.: 'Welcome' – form of greeting

menorah Heb.: candelabrum with seven candlesticks of the ancient Jewish temple in Jerusalem; national symbol of the Jews

milk-brother a foster brother to whom one's mother was wet-nurse. Sometimes a nursing mother fed the child of another who was unable to nurse him herself. Such children are assumed to be related, and cannot marry, for example.

millet system a system of government in the Ottoman Empire whereby non-Muslim communities were organized under a religious head of their own who also exercised important civil functions

moshavim Heb.: plural of *moshav* – a cooperative settlement of individual farms

mukhtar Ar.: village elder

Phalangists a Lebanese Christian militia (mainly Maronite); the name was taken from the Spanish fascist organization of the same name

qassis Ar.: title given to a Protestant priest

Ramadan Ar.: the Muslim holy month in which Muslims fast and refrain from drinking and smoking from dawn to dusk

ruh Allah Ar.: 'the Spirit of God'

Sabra Heb.: name given to Jews born in Israel

shalom Heb.: 'peace', used as a Jewish greeting

sheikh Ar.: title of respect given to the head of a family, tribe or village; Muslim scholar etc.

Shin Beth the Israeli internal security agency

sulha Ar.: lit. peace, reconciliation, settlement; peacemaking. A traditional form of ending disputes among Palestinians

suq Ar.: market

sura Ar.: verse of the Qur'an

ulpanim Hebrew-language schools in Israel

Wafa Palestinian press agency

waqf Ar.: religious endowment; property left in trust to the Church or the Muslim community

appendix one

UN Resolution 181 (II) (excerpts)
29 November 1947

PLAN OF PARTITION WITH ECONOMIC UNION

Part I Future constitution and government of Palestine

1. The Mandate for Palestine shall terminate as soon as possible but in any case not later than 1 August 1948.

2. The armed forces of the mandatory Power shall be progressively withdrawn from Palestine, the withdrawal to be completed as soon as possible but in any case not later than 1 August 1948.

The mandatory Power shall advise the Commission, as far in advance as possible, of its intention to terminate the Mandate and evacuate each area.

The mandatory Power shall use its best endeavours to ensure that an area situated in the territory of the Jewish State, including a seaport and hinterland adequate to provide facilities for a substantial immigration, shall be evacuated at the earliest possible date and in any event not later than 1 February 1948.

3. Independent Arab and Jewish States and the Special International Regime for the City of Jerusalem, set forth in part III of this plan, shall come into existence in Palestine two months after the evacuation of the armed forces of the mandatory Power has been completed but in any case not later than 1 October 1948. The boundaries of the Arab State, the Jewish State and the City of Jerusalem shall be as described in parts II and III below.

4. The period between the adoption by the General Assembly of its recommendation on the question of Palestine and the establishment of the independence of the Arab and Jewish States shall be a transitional period.

Part III City of Jerusalem

The City of Jerusalem shall be established as a *corpus separatum* under a special international regime and shall be administered by the United Nations. The Trusteeship Council shall be designated to discharge the responsibilities of the Administering Authority on behalf of the United Nations.

The City of Jerusalem shall include the present municipality of Jerusalem plus the surrounding villages and towns, the most eastern of which shall be Abu Dis; the most southern, Bethlehem; the most western, Ein Karim (including also the built-up area of Motsa); and the most northern Shu'fat, as indicated on the attached sketch-map (annex B).

The Trusteeship Council shall, within five months of the approval of the present plan, elaborate and approve a detailed Statute of the City which shall contain *inter alia* the substance of the following provisions:

1. *Government machinery; special objectives.* The Administering Authority in discharging its administrative obligations shall pursue the following special objectives:
(a) To protect and to preserve the unique spiritual and religious interests located in the city of the three great monotheistic faiths throughout the world, Christian, Jewish and Moslem; to this end to ensure that order and peace, and especially religious peace, reign in Jerusalem;
(b) To foster co-operation among all the inhabitants of the city in their own interests as well as in order to encourage and support the peaceful development of the mutual relations between the two Palestinian peoples throughout the Holy Land; to promote the security, well-being and any constructive measures of development of the residents, having regard to the special circumstances [of the two] peoples and communities.

UN Resolution 242
22 November 1967

The Security Council,

Expressing its continuing concern with the grave situation in the Middle East,

Emphasising the inadmissibility of the acquisition of territory by war and the need to work for a just and lasting peace in which every State in the area can live in security,

Emphasising further that all Member States in their acceptance of the Charter of the United Nations have undertaken a commitment to act in accordance with Article 2 of the Charter,

1. Affirms that the fulfilment of Charter principles requires the establishment of a just and lasting peace in the Middle East which should include the application of both the following principles:

i. Withdrawal of Israel armed forces from territories occupied in the recent conflict;

ii. Termination of all claims or states of belligerency and respect for, and acknowledgement of the sovereignty, territorial integrity and political independence of every State in the area and their right to live in peace within secure and recognised boundaries, free from threats or acts of force;

2. Affirms further the necessity

(a) For guaranteeing freedom of navigation through international waterways in the area;

(b) For achieving a just settlement of the refugee problem;

(c) For guaranteeing the territorial inviolability and political independence of every State in the area, through measures including the establishment of demilitarised zones;

3. Requests the Secretary-General to designate a Special Representative to proceed to the Middle East to establish and maintain contacts with the States concerned in order to promote agreement and assist efforts to achieve a peaceful and accepted settlement in accordance with the provisions and principles in this resolution;

4. Requests the Secretary-General to report to the Security Council on the progress of the efforts of the Special Representative as soon as possible.

UN Resolution 338
21 October 1973

The Security Council,

1. Calls upon all parties to the present fighting to cease all firing and terminate all military activity immediately, no later than 12 hours after the movement of the adoption of this decision, in the positions they now occupy;

2. Calls upon the parties concerned to start immediately after the cease-fire the implementation of Security Council Resolution 242 (1967) in all of its parts;

3. Decides that, immediately and concurrently with the cease-fire, negotiations start between the parties concerned under appropriate auspices aimed at establishing a just and durable peace in the Middle East.

appendix two

TEXT OF THE RESOLUTION PERTAINING TO REVEREND CANON RIAH ABU EL-ASSAL AND A PALESTINIAN HOMELAND Passed by the House of Bishops Meeting of the Episcopal Church of the US, 15 September 1986 in San Antonio, Texas:

RESOLVED, That this House sends the assurances of its prayers, its greetings, and its support to the Rt Revd Samir Kafity and the Revd Canon Riah Abu El-Assal, and all our sisters and brothers in the Church in Jerusalem and the Middle East; and be it further

RESOLVED, That this House expresses its deep concern regarding the act of withdrawing the passport of Canon Riah, Rector of Christ Episcopal Church in Nazareth; and be it further

RESOLVED, That this House restates its position regarding the rights of persons to free travel and free expression; and be it further

RESOLVED, That this House deplores any action which impedes or circumscribes any priest from the exercise of his or her priestly ministry; and be it further

RESOLVED, That this House makes these declarations as it reaffirms its commitment to a peace process in the Middle East which will issue in a secure, continuing existence of the State of Israel, at peace with a Palestinian homeland; and be it further

RESOLVED, That copies of this resolution be sent to Bishop Kafity and Canon Riah.

appendix three

List of Destroyed Palestinian Villages

Some names appear more than once, because villages in different locations had the same name:

'Allar	Aal Maliha	Al Buteimat
'Alma	Abil Al Qamh	Al Buweiriya Khirbat
'Ammuqa	Abu al Fadl	Al Chabisiya
'Amqa	Abu al Hewawit	Al Faluja
'Aqir	Abu Kishk	Al Haditha
'Aqqur	Abu Ruthe	Al Hamidiya
'Arab asSukkeir	Abu Shusha	Al Hamra
'Artuf	Abu Shusha	Al Haram
'Ein al Ghidyan	Abu Zeina	Al Harawi
'Ein al Mansi	Abu Zureiq	Al Hiqab
'Ein azZeitun	Ad Damun	Al Huseiniya
'Ein Fit	Ad Darbashiya	Al Jaufa Khirbat
'Ein Ghazal	Ad Daweima	Al Jaufa Khirbat
'Ein Haud	Ad Dumeiri	Al Jiya
'Ein Karim	Ajjur	Al Jura
'Eitarun	Al 'Abisiya	Al Jura
'Ibdis	Al 'Azaziyat	Al Kabri
'Imaret Abu Isder	Al 'Ulmaniya	Al Kafrin
'Innaba	Al Arab Ghawarni	Al Kharrar
'Iqrit	Al Arida	Al Kheima
'Iraq Suweidan	Al Azaziyat	Al Kheriya
'Iribbin Khirbat	Al Bassa	Al Kheya
'Islin	Al Bawati	Al Khuneizir
'Ubeidiya	Al Bira	Al Lauz Khirbat
'Umur Khirbat	Al Birwa	Al Malikiya

Al Manawat
Al Manshiya
Al Manshiya
Al Mansi
Al Mansura
Al Mansura
Al Mansura
Al Mansura
Al Mansura
Al Mas'sudiya
Al Masmiya al Kabira
Al Mazar
Al Mazar
Al Mirr
Al Mughar
Al Mujeidal
Al Mukheizin
Al Murassas
Al Muzeiri
Al Qabu
Al Qastal
Al Qubab
Al Qubeiba
Al Qubeiba
Al Qubeiba
Al Qudeiriya
Al Walaja
Al Yahudiya
An Na'ima
An Nabi Yusha'
An Naghnaqiya
An Nahr
An Nufei'at Arab
Ar Ras al Ahmar
Ar Rihaniya
Ar Ruweis
Arab al Fuquara
Ard al Ishra
As Safa
As Safiriya
As Sakhne
As Salihiya

As Samakiya
As Sanbariya
As Sarafand
As Sawalima
As Sindiyana
As Sumeiriya
Ash Shajara
Ash Shawafir
Ash Sheikh Muwannis
Ash Shuna
Ashrafiya
At Tall
At Taqa
At Tina
At Tira
At Tira
At Tira
Az Zanghariya
Az Zawiya
Az Zawiya, Khirbat
Az Zib
Az Zuq al Fauqani
Az Zuq at Tahtani
Azaziyat
Bait Lid, Khirbat
Balad ash Sheikh
Baqa al Gharbiya
Barbara
Barfilya
Barjiyat
Barqa
Barquaya
Bashshit
Batani Gharbi
Batani Sharqi
Beer Tuviya
Beisamun
Beit 'Affa
Beit 'Itab
Beit Dajan
Beit Daras

Beit Far, Khirbat
Beit Haqquba
Beit Jibrin
Beit Jirja
Beit Jiz
Beit Lahm
Beit Mashir
Beit Nabala
Beit Nattif
Beit Shanna
Beit Susin
Beit Thul
Beit Tima
Beit Umm al Meis
Bilin
Bir es Sab'or
Bir Ma'in
Bir Salim
Birein
Biriya
Birkat Ramadan
Biyar 'Adas
Buleida
Buleida
Bureij
Bureika
Bureir
Buweiziya
Dalhamiya, Khirbat
Dallata
Dalyat Ar Rauha
Danna
Danyal
Dawara
Deir 'Amr
Deir Abu Salama
Deir ad Dubban
Deir al Qasi
Deir el Hawa
Deir esh Sheikh
Deir Muheisin

Deir Nakhkhas
Deir Suneid
Deir Tarif
Deir Tasin
Deiraban
Deishum
Dhahiriya et Tahta
Dhuheiriya
Dimra
Ed Daraje
Ein Fit
El Burj
El Burj, Khirbat
El Fatur
El Ghazawiya
El Hamade
El Kunaiyisa
El Maderiya
El Manara
El Metrade
El Muweilih
El W'ara es Sauda
Es Samiriya
Et Tahame
Et Tahame
Eth Themele
Ez Zababida, Khirbat
Fajja
Fara
Fardisya
Farradiya
Farwana
Fir'im
Gat Rimmon
Ghabbatiya
Ghaziya
Ghubaiya al Fauqa
Ghubaiya al Tahta
Ghuraba
Ghuweir Abu Shusha
Hadatha

Hamama
Hatte
Hirbya
Hittin
Huj
Huleiqat
Hunin
Idhnibba
Ijzim
Ikhza' Khirbat
Imsura
Indur
Injeib el ful
Iraq al Manshiya
Isdun
Ishwa
Ismallah
Ja'una
Jaba'
Jabbul
Jahula
Jaladiya
Jalil Al Qibliya
Jalil Ash Shamaliya
Jammama
Jammasin ash Sharqi
Jammasin el Gharbi
Jarash
Jarisha
Jazayir el Hindaj
Jazayir el Hindaj
Jiddin
Jidru
Jilya
Jimzu
Jindas
Jubb Yusuf
Julis
Juseir
Kabara Khirbat
Kafara

Kafar I'nan
Kafr 'Ana
Kafr Bir'im
Kafr Lam
Kafr Saba
Kafra
Karatiya
Kasla
Kaufhakha
Kaukab
Kaukab al Hawa
Kefar Uriya
Khalisa
Khan el Minya
Khirbat ad Damun
Khirbat edh Dhuheiriya
Khirbat Nataf
Khirbat Zakariya
Khisas
Khisas Khirbat
Khiyam al Walid
Khubbeiza
Khulda
Khureish
Kidna
Kirad al Ghannama
Kuweikat
Lajjun
Lazzaza
Lidd Khirbat
Lifta
Lubya
Ma'dhar
Ma'lul
Ma'sub
Majdal
Majdal
Majdal, Khirbat
Majdal Yaba
Mallaha
Manshiya Khirbat

Mansurat al Kheit
Marus
Masmiya as Saghira
Mayat Awad
Meiron
Meis
Mi'ar
Miska
Mughallis
Mughr al Kheit
Mughr ed Druz
Mughr Edduruz
Mughr esh Sha'ban
Muharraqa
Nabi Rubin
Nabi Rubin
Najd
Nasir ed Din
Ni'ana
Ni'ilya
Nimrin
Nugeib
Nuris
Qadas
Qaddita
Qalunya
Qannir
Qastina
Qatra
Qazaza
Qeitiya
Qisariya
Quabba'a
Quaqun
Quira wa Qamun
Qumbaza Khirbat
Qumya
Ra'na
Raml Zeita

Rantiya
Ras Abu 'Ammar
Ras ez Zuwuire
Raud Khattab
Ruweis el Beden
S'umman Khirbat
Sa'sa'
Sabalan
Sabbarin
Saffouriya
Safsaf
Sajad
Salama
Salbit
Salha
Samakh
Sammu'i
Samra
Saqiya
Sara'
Sarafand el 'Amar
Sarafand el Kharab
Saris
Sarona
Sataf
Sawafir al Gharbiya
Sawafir ash Shamalya
Sehel al Hawa
Seidun
Shauqa et Tahta
Shoma
Sirin
Suba
Sufla
Suhmata
Summeil
Sumsum
Suruh
Tabgha

Tabsur
Tall as Safi
Tall ash Shauk
Tantura
Tarbikha
Teitaba
Tell el Hinud
Tuleil
Ulam
Ulm Kolkha
Umm 'Ajr
Umm al Faraj
Umm az Zinat
Umm Burj
Umm esh Shauf
Umm Khalid
Umm Reshrush
Umm Sabuna, Khirbat
Wadi 'Ara
Wadi al Quabbani
Wadi Hunein
Waldheim
Waraquani
Weiziya
Wilhelma
Yajur
Yaquq
Yarda
Yasur
Yazur
Yibna
Yubla
Zab'a
Zakariya
Zalafa Khirbat
Zarnuqa
Zeita
Zikrin
Zir'in

Notes

1 Home sweet home
1 David Ben Gurion, Prime Minister of Israel 1948–53 and 1955–63.

2 Caught in between
1 According to UN Resolution 181: see Appendix 1.
2 The Triangle is an area of land to the south west of Nazareth whose points are marked by the towns Umm El Fahm, Taibeh and Tireh.
3 Sabri Jeryis, *The Arabs in Israel*, The Institute for Palestine Studies, Beirut, 1969.
4 Eli Tabor, *Yediot Ahronot*, 2 November 1982, cited in Noam Chomsky, *The Fateful Triangle*, Pluto Press, London and Sydney, 1983.

3 Present absentees
1 Cited from Noam Chomsky, *The Fateful Triangle*, Pluto Press, London and Sydney, 1983.
2 D. Kretzmer, *The Legal Status of the Arabs in Israel*, Westview Press, Boulder, San Francisco, Oxford, 1990.
3 Revd Jamal had cooperated with the previous mayor, Mayor Y. Fahoum, to dissuade the Palestinians from leaving Nazareth during the fighting in 1948.
4 See Appendix 3 for list of destroyed villages.
5 Sabri Jeryis, *The Arabs in Israel*, The Institute for Palestine Studies, Beirut, 1969.

8 For God's sake
1 *Tzavuot Haganah LeIsrael* = Israeli Defence Forces.
2 Revd Assad Mansour, *A History of Nazareth: Early Days to the Present Day*, Hilal Printing Press, Cairo, 1924, p. 87.

9 How shall they hear without a preacher?
1 Indeed, most Jews who came from the Arab countries speak and understand Arabic. Some estimate that over 50 per cent of the Israeli population speak Arabic.

2 Majid El Haj and Henry Rosenfeld, *Arab Local Government in Israel*, Westview Press, Boulder, San Francisco, Oxford, 1990.

13 A prisoner in my own country

1 For text of the Resolution see Appendix 2.

14 Sulha

See Appendix 1.

Index